Herbal Magick

A Witch's Guide to Herbal Folklore and Enchantments

By

Gerina Dunwich

NEW PAGE BOOKS
A division of The Career Press, Inc.
Franklin Lakes, NJ

Herbal Magick

Edited and typeset by Nicole DeFelice
Cover design by Visual Group
Printed in the U.S.A. by Book-mart Press

To order this title, please call toll-free 1-800-CAREER-1 (NJ and Canada: 201-848-0310) to order using VISA or MasterCard, or for further information on books from Career Press.

The Career Press, Inc., 3 Tice Road, PO Box 687,
Franklin Lakes, NJ 07417

www.careerpress.com
www.newpagebooks.com

Library of Congress Cataloging-in-Publication Data

Dunwich, Gerina.
    Herbal magick : a witch's guide to herbal folklore and enchantments / by Gerina Dunwich.
        p. cm.
    Includes bibliographical references and index.
    ISBN 1-56414-575 (pbk.)
        1. Witchcraft. 2. Herbs—Miscellanea. I. Title.

BF1572.P43 D85 2002
133.4'3—dc21

                                                        2001044650

Also by Gerina Dunwich:

Candlelight Spells
The Magick of Candleburning
{republished as *Wicca Candle Magick*}
The Concise Lexicon of the Occult
Circle of Shadows
Wicca Craft
The Secrets of Love Magick
{republished as *Wicca Love Spells*}
The Wicca Book of Days
The Wicca Garden
The Wicca Source Book
The Wicca Source Book {Revised Second Edition}
The Modern Witch's Complete Source Book
Everyday Wicca
A Wiccan's Guide to Prophecy and Divination
{republished as *The Wiccan's Dictionary of*
Prophecy and Omens}
Wicca A to Z
Magick Potions
Your Magickal Cat
The Pagan Book of Halloween
Exploring Spellcraft
The Cauldron of Dreams

Contents

Foreword

    I am often asked during interviews if I am a "White Witch" or a "Black Witch," which has always brought to mind Glinda asking Dorothy is she is "a good Witch or a bad Witch" in *The Wizard of Oz*. I always reply that if I had to attach a color to myself as a Witch, it would be "Gray." Like Wiccans, I also try to work my spells for the good of others and I seek to harm none. Being a Witch who is rather well known throughout the world due to my numerous published works, I am occasionally approached by individuals seeking to have an enemy or two done away with through magickal means. There was one man from Russia who went as far as to mail me a letter, signed in his own blood, promising to pay me $1000 if I would curse his son's wife to have a miscarriage simply because he disapproved of his son marrying outside of the family's orthodox religion! Despite my being offered some generous amounts of money and expensive gifts in exchange for such services, I have always refused and will continue to do so. I do not believe in using magick for the purpose of doing harm to others, except in extreme cases where it is absolutely necessary for one's own self-defense or survival.

    I firmly believe in magickal self-defense and the teaching of lessons (for the good of others, of course) when they are needed, or when all else fails. If someone tries to inflict harm upon my loved ones or me, I will not hesitate to work my magick to bind or bring down a hex upon them. And if someone dispatches a curse to me, I do not turn the other cheek or take the attitude of "let the gods deal with it." I send it right back to the sender. Those are my personal set of ethics. You may or may not agree with them, which is fine in either case, but I will neither compromise or hide what I believe in for the mere sake of being "politically correct."

The casting of spells involves working with powerful (and often dangerous) magickal energies and is by no means something that should be undertaken by an untrained novice. Whenever working with energies, you should always take care to protect yourself the best you can through the use of magick circles, amulets, talismans, and so forth. You should also be warned that, despite your magickal knowledge and your best efforts, the possibility of any kind of a spell backfiring always exists. This is not an uncommon thing to have happen, and many of the practitioners that I know, including myself, have experienced it at least once. It has nothing to do with karma, displeased gods, or Gerald Gardner's threefold law, despite what some people choose, or are led, to believe. It has everything to do with the instability of magickal energy and/or a practitioner's incorrect application of it.

Within this book you will discover the magickal history of herbs and learn how different Pagan traditions have employed certain plants in their magickal workings and religious rites. Without question, some of the spells contained herein might be viewed as falling within the parameters of what is popularly referred to as "gray," or possibly even "black" magick. However, it is important to remember that the majority of these spells were either borrowed from, or inspired by, a number of centuries-old magickal traditions unrelated to the relatively modern religious movement known as Wicca.

Should you find yourself feeling uneasy about performing any of the spells in this book, you should not hesitate to modify them to suit your particular needs, tradition, ethics, and so forth. Provided that you do not alter any of its basic correspondences, a spell can often be changed without altering its purpose or rendering it completely useless. In fact, I have always been a firm believer that the more you personalize a spell, the better results it will yield for you.

Your other option, obviously, is to simply not use a particular spell that you feel uneasy with or not drawn to. The choice is up to you. However, where ethics lie, I will not decide for you what is right and what is wrong. But I will try to present the pros and cons as honestly and completely as I can so you can make an informed decision for yourself.

With all that being said, it should also be noted here that nearly all Wiccans are strongly opposed to the use of magick (in any form) to manipulate the free will of others, and especially to bring down curses. Although I am not a Wiccan myself, I respect those who adhere to their Wiccan Rede of "harming none." However, I am one Witch who does not pass judgment against my fellow practitioners who may employ the darker forces of magick when they feel that it is absolutely a necessity.

Introduction

Throughout history and throughout the world, herbs have played a major role in magick, religion, superstition, and divination, as well as in the development of humankind.

Witches and Pagan folk the world over have held a special relationship with herbs since the days of antiquity. Developing various methods to harness the magickal energies contained within flowers, leaves, roots, and bark, they have used them as tools for healing, divination, spellcrafting, and connecting with Deity.

The ancients believed that all herbs possessed a spirit, or, as in the case of many poisonous or mind-altering plants, a demon. Nearly every culture has recognized the occult vibrations of herbs, and attributed certain magickal properties to their native plants and trees.

It is said in the *Magic and Medicine of Plants* (Reader's Digest), "Our distant ancestors did not need to be trained botanists to observe and appreciate the remarkable energy and diversity of the plant world."

Early civilizations sought to harness and direct the magickal powers of plants for curing diseases, warding off misfortune, divining the future, and appeasing the gods. In ancient Egypt, a land that has been described as "an ideal breeding ground" for magickal herbalism, plants such as the lotus, the papyrus reed, and the onion (which was often presented as a sacrificial offering to the gods) were greatly revered and believed to possess spiritual virtues.

Despite the fact that myrrh trees were not native to Egypt, myrrh played a vital role in the religious and magickal ceremonies of the ancient Egyptians. The fragrant aroma produced by the burning of myrrh was believed to be pleasing to the gods. Myrrh was burned every day at the midday hour as an offering to the sun god Ra, and was also fumed in the temples where the goddess Isis was worshipped.

The people of ancient Greece and Rome linked their native trees and plants to the gods and goddesses of their pantheons. In the old Greek and Roman religions, plant myths figured predominantly. Tales of mortals and gods alike being transformed into trees were common, and nearly every deity was known to have held one or more tree and/or plant as a sacred symbol.

Historically, belief in the magickal properties of plants was by no means restricted only to Pagans and pre-Christian religions. Numerous references to herbal magick and botanomancy (the art and practice of divination by plants) can be found throughout the Bible, from the burning bush oracle of Moses, to Rachel's use of mandrake roots to magickally increase her fertility, to Jacob's magickal use of striped poplar, almond, and plane-tree rods to bring forth striped, speckled, and spotted livestock offspring.

During the Middle Ages, Witches (or, perhaps more accurately, women and men who were *accused* of being Witches) were believed to have employed a wide variety of plants to bring about evil, as well as to do good if they so desired. Those who made use of poisonous plants such as hemlock and henbane to lay curses or cause mischief were labeled "Black Witches." Those who applied their herbal wisdom for the benefit of others (such as for healing or working love magick) earned for themselves the reputation of a "White Witch" (which was equated to being a good Witch.) Those who were "White Witches" were far more respected in most circles than their "Black" counterparts. But of course not all Witches were exclusively "White" or "Black." Those who practiced a little bit of both were said to be "Gray."

However, as a charge of Witchcraft (regardless of its "color") oftentimes resulted in a death sentence preceded by the most heinous acts of torture, wise Witches of old needed to carefully practice their craft veiled behind the shadows of secrecy.

A great deal of what little botanical witch lore remains from centuries past is contained in the transcripts of the Witchcraft trials that took place during the Burning Times. "From such sources," observe the editors of *Magic and Medicine of Plants*, "we gather that witches were heirs to ancient lessons about the medicinal properties of many substances found in nature. The Witches preserved and continued to use plant lore that the Christian church had suppressed as 'heathen' mysteries."

In the United States, magickal herbalism is largely rooted in European botanical lore brought across the Atlantic by immigrants from distant lands, and influenced to varying degrees by Native American herb lore and the plant magick practiced by African slaves.

In contemporary times, as it has been in the past, herbal magick remains an essential part of the Witches' craft. It can be used to assist an individual in attracting a compatible lover, landing the right job, changing bad luck into good, and even increasing one's wealth! Empowered by the energies of Goddess Earth and her elementals, herbs have long been used as amulets to protect against evil, dried and burned as magickal incense during rituals, and added to flying ointments and cauldron brews.

Herbs can be used to cure or to curse, as well as to conjure or to banish supernatural entities. They can enchant our gardens and our homes, and guide us on the path to transformation and self-improvement. But, most importantly, herbal magick can open the door to spiritual realms and other worlds, and serve to connect a human being with Mother Nature and the Divine.

There probably exists no plant or tree that hasn't at one time, in some part of the world, been used in a spell or potion, or utilized as an amulet. And it is said that all parts of a plant, whether they be roots, buds, flowers, stems, or bark, are magickally significant.

Herbs are Mother Nature's gifts to all of humankind, regardless of spiritual beliefs, magickal tradition, or culture. And whether you pride yourself as a country Witch or an urban Pagan, herbs can reward you with a wealth of enchantment, divination, and folklore.

Blessed be!

Chapter 1:
Pagan Herb Lore

Magickal Memories of Grandma Rose

My beloved Grandma Rose came to the United States from Italy when she was but a young woman. After living in New York for many years, she relocated with her husband and grown children to the quaint village of Riverside, Illinois. She lived the remainder of her 85 years there in a magnificent red brick house that had been built in the Colonial Revival style with a stately semicircular entrance porch flanked by white Ionic columns.

From its cobwebbed attic filled with dusty old trunks and restless spirits, to its white and black tiled 1940's-styled kitchen that was ever filled with the sweet aroma of Italian seasonings and butter cookies, Grandma Rose's house grew to be a very special place for me as I was growing up. It was there that I attended my first séance, had my first psychic experience, learned about Witchcraft, and was initiated into the Craft by my older cousin Carol, who was a White Witch.

Grandmother's Garden

Grandma Rose enjoyed gardening and had a special way with plants. Her talent was what some would call a "green thumb." The grounds behind her house hosted a beautiful garden filled with roses, vegetables, fruit trees, and herbs.

I have many fond childhood memories of my grandmother's garden, and to me it was quite an enchanted place. Sometimes it seems as though it was only yesterday that I walked barefoot upon its dew-kissed violets and clover on a misty summer morning or smelled the scent of its parsley, basil, and oregano plants, as I lay upon a hammock reading omens in the clouds drifting lazily above.

Fairies and other nature spirits were said to have inhabited Grandma Rose's fragrant and secluded garden. I never actually saw them, but I could always sense their nearby presence whenever I spent time there. Sometimes I would catch a glimpse of some tiny sparkling thing moving in my peripheral vision, but as soon as I would turn to look, it would always be gone.

I also remember an old tree near the garden that my friends and I felt was inhabited by some unseen elfin creature (for lack of a better word). They feared that tree and always kept their distance from its grotesquely twisted trunk and branches whenever we'd play in the yard. But, for some reason, I always felt strangely drawn to it and would often tell my secrets to it or place flowers or some of my toys at its base as gifts for the elemental spirit dwelling within.

Grandma's Home Remedies

My grandmother was a wise woman. She knew of the healing powers that herbs possessed and often applied them in her home remedies. Garlic was revered for treating infections, homemade apple cider vinegar for the itching caused by poison ivy, and witch hazel for swellings and inflammations. When my mother was a young girl and was stricken with rheumatic fever, Grandma Rose treated her with a mustard poultice that she called a plaster.

I later learned that mustard seeds possessed not only medicinal value, but magickal ones as well. In the rural regions of
the "old country," as my grandmother often called her home-
land of Italy, it was a common folk custom to sprinkle black
mustard seeds on the windowsills and thresholds of dwellings
in order to prevent restless ghosts and evil spirits from gaining
entrance.

I was very close to my Grandma Rose when I was growing
up. Nearly every afternoon after school let out for the day, my
mother would pick me up and we'd drive over to my
grandmother's house in Riverside to visit her and help her out
with her grocery shopping, household chores, and the preparation of dinner. Crippling arthritis had immobilized both of
Grandma Rose's legs, making it both painful and difficult for
her to walk or stand for any long length of time. She appreci-
ated the help and greatly enjoyed the company.

The Evil Eye

Grandma Rose would spend hours upon end talking to
my mother about such things as old family recipes, folk remedies, and the "good old days" of her youth spent in far away
Italy. Every so often I would overhear her speak of the *mal
occhio* (the evil eye), especially whenever a certain woman who
had a reputation as being the neighborhood gossip became
the topic of conversation.

I don't know whether or not Grandma Rose actually believed in the powers of the evil eye, but it was a subject that
she enjoyed talking about and appeared to be quite well versed
in. She said there were people known in Italy as *jettatore* (individuals who possessed the *mal occhio*). To cast their curse upon
another, all they needed to do was gaze enviously upon that
person, often while praising them. In some cases, an angry, venomous stare would be the only thing needed to work the magick.

However, not every *jettatore* was aware of the fact that he or she possessed the evil eye, and they would often cast it upon their victims involuntarily and without a deliberate malicious intent behind it. There was no explanation why certain people were born with it and others were not, but it was clear that not all persons who were capable of casting it were evil by nature.

Such was the case of Pope Pius IX, who many Italians believed was a *jettatore*. Although he was not considered to be a malevolent man, the curious fact that unexplained disasters befell a great number of the persons and places blessed by him led many folks to believe that such a thing could not be a mere coincidence. The only acceptable explanation for them was that he possessed the *mal occhio*.

The Italians have many methods of combating the evil eye. Most are simple ones, such as spitting on the ground, wearing red ribbons, reciting certain passages from the Bible, and making phallic hand gestures. The wearing of a golden charm shaped like a horn and filled with a pinch of sage is another method that is said to be highly effective against the evil eye, and one that continues to remain popular among many Italians. In fact, I have two male relatives on the Italian side of my family who frequently wear such a charm on a gold necklace. While neither of them will readily admit to believing in the power of the evil eye, they evidently feel that it is far better to be safe than to be sorry. And I couldn't agree with them more.

Some methods involve the use of herbs, many of which Grandma Rose grew in her garden and kept in mason jars in her walk-in pantry. Anise seeds could ward off the evil eye by being burned or strewn around the home. The ancient Romans believed that eating rue could give them immunity against the evil eye, while bathing one's eyes with water in which rue had been steeped was supposedly effective in curing those who had already fallen victim to a *jettatore's* evil glance.

The ritual burning of frankincense, myrrh, and sandalwood was, at one time, believed by many magickally-minded individuals to be a highly effective method for diverting the evil eye. These, and other fragrant botanicals, would also be strewn around the home to prevent persons who possessed the evil eye from gaining entry and causing harm. This method was also thought to be a preventative against the evil eye, as well as a means of inducing second sight.

To protect yourself against the malevolent power of the evil eye, wear or carry a mojo bag filled with one or more of the following herbs: angelica, betony leaves, anise (also known as aniseed), castor beans, henna, lady's slipper, lavender (nicknamed "elf leaf" by Pagan folk of centuries past), lime tree twigs, pennyroyal, periwinkle, rue, sage.

"The glances of envy and malice do shoot also subtilly; the eye of the malicious person does really infect and make sick the spirit of the other." —John Aubrey, 1696.

Olde Wives' Tales

The numbers of superstitious beliefs concerning herbs and trees abound, and there are probably enough of them to fill several large volumes. These "olde wives' tales" (as some like to call them) can be found in just about every part of the world, and they have been with us practically since the dawn of humankind.

In my younger years, I knew a very religious Christian girl who held firmly onto the belief that the Almighty Lord had cursed the soil of the earth with weeds as punishment to Adam and Eve for failing to obey His command. I am also acquainted with several people who believe that the more weeds a person has growing in her yard, the worse off her luck will be!

I learned about herbal superstitions and the reading of plant omens early in life. My mother once told me that it is not uncommon for a houseplant to wither and lose its leaves should its owner become seriously ill or pass away. She also believed that the sudden death of a healthy, well cared for houseplant was a very bad sign, indicating that a grave illness or even a death in the family was in the offing.

Someone once told me that a lightning-struck tree also presages ill health or, in some cases, death for a member of the household upon whose land the tree stands. Cutting down a healthy tree, especially if it is an oak (sacred to the ancient Druid priests), has long been regarded by many folks as a most unlucky thing to do.

I remember a very old oak tree that once stood behind my childhood home, and how I adored the radiant colors of its leaves each year when autumn came to the Midwest. One afternoon, a tree trimming crew armed with their chainsaws was working their way down the street where my family and I lived, cutting all the tree branches that had grown into the telephone and power lines. One of the tree trimmers came to our front door and inquired if my mother was interested in having the old oak tree in our backyard removed. Her reply was a firm "no," but this man was persistent and attempted to convince her that the tree should be cut down because it was so old and overgrown. Angrily, my feisty Taurean mother told him that it would be bad luck to harm that tree and that a curse would befall anyone who dared to cut it down while it was still alive. She then bid him good afternoon and shut the door.

Years later, we sold our house to a family who wasted no time in cutting down our beloved oak tree so that a wooden fence could be put up around the backyard for their dog. It saddened me to learn of the dreadful fate that had befallen the mighty oak that once towered so majestically outside my bedroom window, and since then I've wondered from time to time if the old superstition of the oak tree's curse ever came to be.

"Superstitions are instinctive, and all that is instinctive is founded in the very nature of things, to which fact the skeptics of all times have given insufficient attention."

—Eliphas Levi, *The Doctrine and Ritual of Magic.*

Lucky and Unlucky Herbs

The following plants, according to Scott Cunningham, possess the power to attract good luck: allspice, aloe vera, bamboo, banyan, be-still, bluebell, cabbage, calamus, Chinaberry, cinchona, cotton, daffodil, devil's-bit, ferns, grains of paradise, hazel, holly, houseleek, huckleberry, Irish moss, Job's tears, linden, lucky hand root, moss, nutmeg, oak, orange, persimmon, pineapple, pomegranate, poppy, purslane, rose, snakeroot, star anise, straw, strawberry, sumbul, vetivert, violet, and wood rose.

Additionally, rosemary and St. John's wort are said to bring good luck to a home, as well as to drive out demons and ghosts. But the two luckiest plants to bring indoors, according to English herb lore, are white heather and rowan tree.

In the Welsh countryside, as well as in other parts of the world, it is believed that bad luck will befall any person who dares to pick a leaf or flower growing atop a grave.

It was once widely believed among country folk that it was unlucky to bring into the house a bunch of primroses or daffodils totaling any number less than 13. Doing so was said to have an adverse effected upon the fertility of chickens and geese, causing them to lay fewer eggs.

It is extremely unlucky to bring blackthorn into the house. A blossoming branch from this plant is believed by some folks to precipitate an illness or death in the family when brought indoors.

Hydrangea planted near the house or brought indoors will curse your daughters with spinsterhood, and parsley (if it is given as a gift) will impart the worst of luck to both the giver and the recipient.

Other plants said to invite bad luck when brought into a house include broom (especially if brought in during the month of May), dog rose, elder, gorse (also known as furze flower), hawthorn, heather (unless it is white), ivy, lilac, lily-of-the-valley, pussy willow, snowdrops, and the flowers of any plant, shrub, or tree (especially fruit-bearing ones) that bloom out of season.

> *"Hawthorn blooms and elder flowers,*
> *Fill a house with evil powers."*
> —An old English saying.

The speedwell was once thought to be an unlucky flower. So unlucky, in fact, many young children were often warned not to gather it lest their mothers would die before the year was done. In some parts of England, it is still believed by some that picking speedwell (also known as "bird's-eye") will cause one's eyes to be pecked out by birds!

Bringing any type of white flowers into the house will result in a death in the family, according to an old superstition. To avoid bad luck, white flowers should never be given to the ill or brought into hospitals.

Bringing yew into one's home is also said to be a very unlucky thing to do. Some folks believe that if it is brought indoors at Christmas, a family member will meet his or her demise within the next 12 months.

Herbs of the Devil

As any contemporary Witch, Neo-Pagan, or educated occult historian can tell you, worship of the Christian's devil was never an element of the Old Religion or the Witches' Craft. However, the vast majority of Christians in the Middle Ages believed otherwise. They viewed all Witches as being in league with the Prince of Darkness, and were convinced that it was from him that the Witches received their evil powers. This had a big impact in the area of herbal folklore, as many of the plants used both magickally and medicinally by Witches became forever linked to the devil and branded with diabolical nicknames that reflected this.

The following is a list of plants, beginning with their common names or botanical names (in italics) and followed by their nicknames relating to the devil:

Alaskan ginseng: devil's club

Alstonia scholaris: devil's tree

Asafoetida: devil's dung

Bachelor's buttons: devil's flower

Belladonna: devil's cherries

Bindweed: devil's guts

Cassytha spp: devil's twine

Celandine: devil's milk

Colicroot: devil's-bit

Datura: devil's apple

Dill: devil-away

Dodder: devil's guts; devil's hair; hellweed

Elder: devil's eye

Elephant's foot: devil's grandmother

Fairywand: devil's bit

False (or white) hellebore: devil's bite; devil's tobacco

Fern: devil's bush

Field convolvulus: devil's weed

Grapple plant: devil's claw root

Hedge bindweed: devil's vine

Henbane: devil's eye

Hieracium aurantiacum: devil's paintbrush

Indigo berry: devil's pumpkin
Jimsonweed: devil's-apple; devil's trumpet
Lambertia formosa: mountain devil
Mandrake: Satan's apple
Mayapple: devil's-apple
Mexican poppy: devil's fig
Mistletoe: devil's fuge
Parsley: devil's oatmeal
Periwinkle: devil's eye
Pothos: devil's ivy
Pricklypear cactus: devil's-tongue
Puffball fungus: devil's snuffbox
Queen Anne's lace: devil's plague
Viper's bugloss: bluedevil
Wild yam: devil's-bones
Yarrow: devil's nettle

There is a rather curious legend, which dates back to medieval times, about how the plant known as the devil's-bit (*Succisa pratensis*) came to receive its devilish name. It holds that when humankind discovered this plant's thick, tapered root was effective in treating many of the ailments that the devil and his minions took great delight in afflicting upon the mortal race, the devil became so infuriated that he took an angry bite out of the plant's root. This resulted in the root's gnashed appearance, which in turn led to its name. A similar legend about the devil is connected to the colicroot (*Aletris farinosa*), which is also known as devil's-bit (in addition to numerous other folk names).

In medieval Europe, oregano was believed to be highly effective in warding off sorcerers, demons, snakes, and venomous animals. Any person who carried oregano as an herbal amulet could neither be harmed nor tempted by the devil.

During the Burning Times, it was a common practice for many inquisitors to burn oregano twigs during the torture sessions of accused Witches. It was believed that the smoke generated by burning oregano effectively kept the devil from aiding his servants.

Parsley was another plant associated with the devil in centuries past. Notorious for its incredibly slow germination, parsley seed was said by some to have to go seven times to hell to obtain the devil's permission before it could grow. Others believed that it had to go to the devil nine times before coming up. According to a related superstition, if parsley seeds failed to germinate, the unfortunate individual who planted them would meet with death sometime within the coming year.

Many devil-fearing folks regard St. John's wort as the most potent herbal amulet against Satan, as well as all things of an evil nature. In Great Britain, it was once common for St. John's wort to be sewn into one's garments for protection against the devil. To keep homes and their inhabitants safe from the evils and mischief of the devil and his fiends, it was customary for sprigs of St. John's wort to be gathered on St. John's Eve and then hung over the doors and windows.

To drive away "phantastical spirits," according to Robert Burton's 17th-century work, *The Anatomy of Melancholy*, St. John's wort should be gathered on a Friday and then "hung about the neck."

It was not uncommon for children in the 17th century to be made to wear a piece of mistletoe on a necklace for protection against the devil and evil spirits. Many superstitious folks of that period also employed mistletoe as a charm against demonic possession.

It is said that if you cast yarrow upon your doorstep, the devil will dare not enter your house. This procedure is also recommended for keeping out evil spirits and negativity, as well as averting both bad luck and wicked spells.

Centuries ago in England, it was believed that burning the wood of the elder (a tree said to have been used by the

Druids to both bless and curse) invited the devil into one's home. However, hanging elder over the doors and windows works to keep him out.

Holly (once known as the "holy bush") and yews were frequently planted near houses and in churchyards during the Middle Ages in the belief that they kept the devil and his legion of demons well at bay.

In Fenland (a community in the East of England), monkey puzzle trees are often found to have been planted in or near graveyards. Said to be disliked by "Old Scratch," these trees are believed to prevent the devil from gaining entry to hallowed burial grounds and claiming the souls of those being laid to rest.

While monkey puzzle trees may not be to the devil's liking, nuts, on the other hand, are something of which he is said to be quite fond. According to an old legend, the devil goes "nutting" every year on "Holy-Rood Day" (September 14th). In the year 1670, the following was published in *Poor Richard's Almanack*: "Let not thy son go a nutting on Holie-Rood day, for fear he meet a tall man in black with cloven feet, which may scare him worse than a rosted [roasted] shoulder of mutton will do a hungrie man." Legend also has it that if a person goes to gather nuts on a Sunday, he or she will have the devil as a companion.

Herbs Associated with Supernatural Creatures

The following is a list of plants, beginning with their common names or botanical names (in italics), and followed by their nicknames relating to fairies, dragons, and other mythological and supernatural creatures.

Ague root: unicorn root
Arisaema (wakerobin): dragon tail
Arisaema draconitium: dragon's-head
Bistort: dragonwort
Calliandra eriophylla: fairy duster
Calochortus albus: white fairy lantern
Calochortus amabilis: green fairy lantern
Calypso bulbosa: fairy slipper
Cat tail: fairy woman's spindle
Cephalanthera austiniae: phantom orchid
Ceratopteris spp: water sprite
Cowslip: fairy cup
Daemomorops draco: dragon's blood
Datura: ghost flower
Devil's bit: false unicorn root
Digitalis: (see Foxglove)
Disporum smithii: coast fairy bells
Dracaena spp: dragon's blood
Draconis resina: dragon's blood
Dracunulus vulgaris: dragon root
Elecampane: elf dock; elfwort
Elm: elven
Epipogium aphyllum: ghost orchid
Eucalyptus papuana: ghost gum
Foxglove: fairy fingers; fairy petticoats; fairy thimbles;
        fairy weed; folk's gloves
Juncus effuses: unicorn
Lavender: elf leaf; silver ghost
Molukka bean: fairy's eggs
Moringa ovalifolia: phantom tree
Mohavea confertiflora: ghost flower
Peristeria elata: ghost orchid

Polypompholyx: fairy aprons
Primula malacoides: fairy primrose
Proboscidea louisianica: unicorn plant
Proserpinaca pectinata (water milfoil): mermaid-weed
Ragwort: fairies' horses
Rosemary: elf leaf
Toadflax: dragon bushes
Wood sorrel: fairy bells
Zephyranthes: fairy lily

Beltane Lore

According to old Pagan tradition, a bonfire that blazes on a Beltane sabbat must be made from nine different kinds of wood, and three pieces of each kind must be used. The following nine types of wood are ideal for use in a sacred Beltane fire. Their traditional meanings are included:

Birch: symbolizes the Goddess or female principle.
Oak: symbolizes the Horned God or male principle.
Rowan: symbolizes life.
Willow: symbolizes death.
Hawthorn: symbolizes purification.
Hazel: symbolizes wisdom.
Apple: symbolizes love.
Vine: symbolizes joy.
Fir: symbolizes immortality and rebirth.

Midsummer Herb Lore

The traditional cutting of mistletoe on Midsummer's Day (June 24th) is a Pagan ritual that originated with the ancient Druids. They believed that the mystical powers associated with this parasitic plant were at their peak on this particular day of the year. The sixth day of the new moon was another time when the plant's powers were believed to be most potent.

The rite called for the herb to be cut with a single stroke of a gold sickle, and it was strictly forbidden for the plant to make contact with the ground. Properly harvested mistletoe was believed to hold abundant healing and divinatory powers.

Another plant with a strong link to Midsummer is Saint John's wort. In the Middle Ages, Europeans who felt a need for protection against demons, ghosts, and sorcerers would gather up Saint John's wort every year on Midsummer, dry the flowers and leaves over their Midsummer fires, and then hang them in small bunches over the doors and windows of their homes, stables, and markets.

Saint John's wort gathered on Midsummer or on a Friday was once believed by some herbalists to cure melancholia (depression) and prevent madness when worn as a charm around the patient's neck. In addition, the plant was reputed to cure or prevent fevers, colds, and a wide variety of other ailments.

Vervain, which is often called the "enchanter's plant" in reference to its diverse magickal attributes and centuries-old affiliation with folk magick, is traditionally gathered on Midsummer or at the rising of the Dog Star when neither the sun nor the moon are visible. Many traditionalists believe that only at these times will the plant be effective for magickal, amuletic, or divinatory purposes.

In medieval times it was widely believed that a chicory plant harvested with a gold blade at noon or at the witching hour on Midsummer gave sorcerers the power to become invisible at will. It was also reputed to unlock any door or box by its insertion into the keyhole or by being rubbed against the lock.

Carrying a handkerchief anointed with the sap of a flowering dogwood tree on Midsummer's Eve is said to work as a charm to make one's wishes come true. I cannot guarantee that everything you desire will materialize for you if you do this. But, as the old expression goes, "be careful what you wish for" just the same!

For protection against sorcery, demons, and the harmful gaze of the evil eye, many folks in the Middle Ages would pass figwort plants through the smoke of a Midsummer fire and then hang them over the doors and windows of their homes as amulets. Legend has it that the figwort possesses great protective powers.

Jumping through the smoke generated by wood betony cast into a Midsummer bonfire is one old Pagan method of purifying the body of demons and disease. Wood betony that is gathered on Midsummer is also believed to have protective powers. It is often kept beneath the pillow to preserve sleepers from nightmares, and worn as an herbal amulet to ward off evil.

Another curious old legend surrounding the Midsummer fire claims that if you gaze into one while looking through a bouquet of larkspur, this will prevent blindness or ailments of the eyes from occurring. The protective power of this spell, however, only remains in effect for one year and the spell must be repeated every Midsummer.

Midsummer is not only a time for working herbal magick, but herbal divinations as well. One old method to make the vision of one's future husband or wife materialize called for a handful of hemp seeds to be sprinkled while walking nine times clockwise around a church and reciting a special incantation. In order for the divination to work, it needed to be carried out at the midnight hour as Midsummer began.

Diviners have employed herbs since ancient times. However, not all herbal divinations center on romance and matrimony. Meadowsweet gathered on Midsummer, for example, was used long ago to determine the gender of a thief. It was believed that if the plant sank when placed on water, the thief was male. If it floated, this indicated a female.

Esbat of the Wort Moon

An Esbat is a monthly Witches' gathering or coven meeting that takes place 13 times a year when the moon is full.

The full moon that occurs during the month of July is known as the wort (or wyrt) moon. However, some folks apply this name to the full moon of August. The word *wort* is old Anglo Saxon for "herb" or "green plant." As the wort moon of July waxes, this is the traditional time for many Pagans to go out into the garden or woods and gather herbs for magickal and/or medicinal use.

An Esbat of the wort moon is an appropriate time for wortcunning (the knowledge and use of the healing and magickal properties of herbs). Many covens, as well as solitaries, dedicate this night to the ritual charging of herbs prior to their preparation and storage. It is also an ideal time for making herbal spell candles, herbal oils, and incense, as well as performing herb-related magick, and giving thanks and presenting offerings, to the spirits that dwell in and watch over a Witch's herb garden. As you place an offering in the garden beneath the rays of the wort moon bright, the spirits may come forth from their secret hiding places among the shadows and reveal to you the many secrets of magickal herbalism.

Chapter 2:
Herbal Superstitions
A to Z

"Superstition is one of the mainsprings of human behaviour, generating hopes of defeating the forces of evil, and of influencing one's own fate." —Iona Opie and Moira Tatem, *A Dictionary of Superstitions.*

Acorn

It was once believed that an acorn placed on a windowsill guarded a house against fires and damage caused by lightning strikes. This superstition can be traced back to the old Norse legend that the great god Thor once sheltered from a thunderstorm under a mighty oak tree.

Adder's Tongue

The British once believed that adder's tongue gathered during the waning of the moon possessed the power to cure adder bites and, according to David Pickering's *Dictionary of Superstitions,* countered "other evils associated with snakes."

Agrimony

According to a rhyme found in a medieval medical manuscript, "If it [agrimony] be leyd under a man's head, he shall sleep as if he were dead. He shall never drede nor waken, till from under his head it be taken."

Almond

According to the ancient Roman author Pliny, the eating of five nuts from an almond tree before drinking wine will work to prevent drunkenness!

If success in your business ventures is what you desire, one way to attain this (in addition to hard work) is to climb to the top of an almond tree, so sayeth an old legend from Asia.

Angelica

Associated with Saint Michael the Archangel, angelica was once thought to dispel lustful thoughts and protect against sorcery, the Black Death, attacks by rabid and venomous beasts, and a wide variety of illnesses.

Apple Tree

If the sun shines on Christmas morning and rain falls on Saint Swithin's Day (July 15th), these are both a good omen that the apple orchards will yield a bountiful crop the following season. To ensure that an apple tree bears fruit for many years, an old custom from Germany is for the first fruit of the season to be consumed by a woman who has bore many children.

There exist a number of death omens related to apple trees. For instance, if there should be a single apple left on a tree after the rest of the crop has been picked at harvesting time and it does not fall to the ground before the arrival of the following spring, the family upon whose land the apple tree stands will lose one of its loved ones to the Angel of Death. Interestingly, it is an old Pagan custom in some parts of the world to deliberately leave one apple on the tree at harvesting time as an offering to the spirits. Beware of apple trees that blossom out of season (particularly in the fall), for they are said to presage a death in the family.

Unicorns, according to Pagan folklore, often dwell beneath apple (and ash) trees. Every so often, one or more of these magnificent magickal creatures can be observed eating or wandering about in an apple orchard, especially in the wee morning hours when the countryside is shrouded in a ghostly mist.

Other apple superstitions are as follows: Eating an apple a day is said to "keep the doctor away." Wassailing apple trees on Twelfth Night keeps all manners of evil spirits at bay. Cutting down an apple orchard is said by some to bring bad luck, and many Pagan folks in Norway once believed that by eating apples they could attain "immortality through wisdom." According to an issue of *Notes and Queries* from the year 1862, "a good apple year is a great year for twins."

Rubbing an apple before eating it is an old method to ensure that the fruit will be free of any evil spirits or demonic entities. Some superstitious folks still believe that if you eat an apple without first rubbing or washing it, you invite the devil to dine with you.

Blackberry

In England, it was once believed that bad luck would befall anyone who dared to pick the fruit of the blackberry plant after the 11th day of October (the old date of the Christian's Feast of Michael-mas). Legend has it that on this day many eons ago the devil fell into a thorny blackberry thicket and laid a curse upon the plant.

Broom

The broom has long been regarded as a plant of ill omen, and unluckiest during the month of May. To sweep the house with blossomed broom in May (or even to bring it into the house) is said to "sweep the head of the house away." In England, it was once believed that the whipping of a young boy with a branch of green broom would result in the stunting of his growth.

Daffodil

If the very first daffodil you lay your eyes upon in the spring or summer hangs its head towards you, this is said to be an omen of bad luck for the remainder of the year. This herbal superstition, which is centuries old, continues to live on in many parts of Great Britain.

Garlic

The legendary power of garlic to keep bloodthirsty vampires and all evil spirits at bay is known throughout much of the world. However, some say that only garlic gathered in the month of May can be truly effective for this purpose.

According to an old legend popular among Christians, the first garlic sprang up in the spot where the Devil's left foot stepped when he left the Garden of Eden. In the spot where his right foot stepped, sprang the first onion.

Garlic is said to be able to absorb the diseases of both man and beast, as well as to trap and destroy negative vibrations and evil influences within cursed or haunted dwellings. (Interestingly, onions are accredited with having the same powers.)

Hawthorn

Also known as hagthorn (due to its long association with Witches), the hawthorn is a very magickal tree that is said to be sacred to the Pagan deities Cardea, Flora, and Hymen. In England it was once believed that the hawthorn was one of the three trees most sacred to the fairy-folk (the others being the oak and the ash).

It is customary for many modern Witches to decorate their Beltane altars and May poles with hawthorn. In ancient times, many a superstitious soul believed that hawthorns were actually Witches in disguise. Many Witches were thought to have been able to transform themselves into trees at will by means of magickal spells, or (according to Christians) through the aid of the devil. Others were said to have danced so wildly around the hawthorns in their frenzied rites that they permanently became as one with the tree.

Take care not to sit beneath the boughs of a hawthorn tree on Halloween (the time of year when the invisible veil between the human and supernatural realms is thinnest), otherwise, you may fall under a fairy enchantment. Cutting down a hawthorn tree is said to greatly anger the fairies, and therefore brings the worst of luck to the one who fells it.

There exist contradicting legends concerning the bringing of hawthorn blossoms into the house. One holds that the blossoms are beneficial, offering the household protection against evil, sorcery, and lightning. Another claims that they are extremely unlucky and may even bring about a death in the family.

Hellebore

Since medieval times, it has been believed that bad luck awaits those who pick the black hellebore. White hellebore flowers, on the other hand, were once believed to cure madness, promote intelligence, and protect against epileptic seizures, leprosy, miscarriages, and attacks by rabid animals.

Long ago, many farmers blessed their cattle with hellebore to protect them against sorcery, and it was for this purpose that the plant was dug up with certain mystical rites. In *The Complete Book of Herbs* by Kay N. Sanecki, it is said that "a circle was described with the point of a sword around the plant, and then prayers were offered while the black roots were lifted."

Some farmers still believe that a good harvest is portended whenever a hellebore plant bears four tufts. However, it is believed to be an extremely bad sign should it bear only two. This portends a crop failure in the near future.

Holly

Known by many names, including "bat's wings" and "Christ's thorn," the holly is a plant strongly connected to the Yuletide season and highly valued by Witches for its magickal and divinatory powers. It was once believed to safeguard a house and its inhabitants against lightning strikes, evil entities, hauntings, and black magick when planted near the dwelling.

Carrying a wand or walking stick made of holly wood will prevent you from falling victim to all hexes and bewitchments, according to occult folklore.

To avoid bad luck, be sure never to bring holly into your house prior to Christmas Eve. However, not having holly in your house at all on Christmas Day is said to conjure the worst of luck for all members of the family.

It is supposed to be very unlucky to step on a holly berry, cut down a holly tree, sweep a chimney with holly, or burn discarded holly boughs, which some folks believe invites the Angel of Death to claim a member of the family.

The so-called "male" variety of holly (with prickly leaves) brings good luck to all persons of the male gender; while the "female" variety (with smooth leaves) brings good luck to all of the fairer sex.

An old Christian legend holds that the cross on which Jesus Christ was crucified was made of holly wood, and it was the blood of Christ that gave the holly berry its deep red color.

It is said that lightning will never strike a holly tree nor anyone who stands under the branches of one during a storm.

It was a widespread belief in the Middle Ages that the holly possessed miraculous curative powers. Pricking or thrashing the feet with holly and then walking barefoot in the snow was once thought to cure chilblains (an inflammatory swelling caused by cold and poor circulation). Another old method for treating chilblains was to rub the ashes of burnt holly berries upon the afflicted areas. To prevent a fever, scratch your legs with a holly branch; and to ease a whooping cough, drink a bit of fresh milk out of a cup or bowl made of holly wood.

Houseleek

In many parts of Great Britain it is still believed that houseleeks growing on the outside walls and/or roof of a house bring phenomenal good luck to all inhabitants of the dwelling. However, should you purposely or accidentally cut down a houseleek, you will suffer a streak of bad luck, especially where your house is concerned.

Houseleeks are also said to protect a house against lightning strikes, fire, and tempests. For this reason, it is traditional for many folks upon moving into a new home to plant them as close to the house as possible before doing anything else. It is also very common for many Welsh families who dwell within thatch-roofed cottages to plant houseleeks upon their rooftops for good luck.

Hydrangea

According to old English folklore, the hydrangea is an unlucky plant for young ladies who wish to find a husband. Persons who allow the plant to grow near their houses (especially close to the front door) are said to curse their daughters with a lonely life of spinsterhood.

Ivy

Some people believe that bringing an ivy plant into the house also brings in bad luck. Picking a leaf from an ivy plant growing on the wall of a church will cause you to fall ill. Even worse, should the ivy growing on the wall of a house suddenly wither and die for no apparent reason, this is said to indicate that a death will occur in that household within a very short time.

Leaves

If the wind should blow leaves of any type into your house, this is said to be a very lucky omen. Catching a falling autumn leaf before it reaches the ground also brings good luck, and some people claim that for every leaf you catch you will have a day filled with good luck. Another superstition holds that if you secretly make a wish as you catch a falling leaf on Halloween, it will surely come true for you. And yet another leaf-catching superstition promises 12 consecutive months of good luck and happiness for those who catch 12 falling leaves in the month of October.

Mandrake

It was once believed that mandrake plants were inhabited by dark-skinned supernatural beings known as *mandragoras* ("man-dragons"), which were mischievous by nature and often called upon to aid sorcerers and sorceresses in the practice of their craft.

A legend dating back to medieval times claims that when a mandrake plant is pulled from the ground, it emits an ear-piercing scream and begins to sweat droplets of blood. Legend also has it that any person whose ears were unfortunate enough to hear the plant's shriek would either be driven to madness or suffer an agonizing death. How this legend came to be is somewhat of a mystery, but it was nevertheless well known throughout Europe and even prompted many practitioners of sorcery to use dogs to uproot their mandrakes as a safety precaution.

One interesting theory concerning the origin of the shrieking mandrake legend can be found in Richard Lucas' *The Magic of Herbs in Daily Living*:

"Tests conducted by Sir Janghadish showed that a plant pulled up by the roots suffers tremendous shock, comparable to that of a person beaten into insensibility. This immediately calls to mind the legend of the screaming mandrake. Perhaps the myth originated when some person here and there with mediumistic ability tore a mandrake from the ground and psychically sensed the plant's torment and anguish. Such an experience would have excited profound emotions of horror in the mind of the psychic, especially if the person was a timid soul or one whose psychic faculties had just emerged for the first time. It is not difficult to understand that in some instances the shock could have caused insanity or heart failure."

Mistletoe

In order to be effective in magickal spells, mistletoe must be cut with a single stroke of a gold sickle on the Summer Solstice, the Winter Solstice, or the sixth day after the new moon. Take care not to let the plant touch the earth, lest it be rendered magickally impotent.

This old Pagan custom originated with the priestly caste of the Celts, who believed that mistletoe found growing on oak trees possessed the power to heal as well as to promote fertility and protect against all manner of evil.

The Druids believed that it was necessary to appease the gods by sacrificing a pair of white bulls during their mistletoe-cutting ritual.

Also known in earlier times as all heal, devil's fuge, golden bough, and Witches' broom, the mistletoe is said to be sacred to the Pagan deities Apollo, Freya, Frigga, Odin, and Venus.

According to old Pagan herb lore, mistletoe works well to ward off lightning strikes and storms when hung from the chimney or over the doors and windows of a dwelling.

Fairies are also said to be repelled by the sight and smell of mistletoe, a belief that unquestionably gave birth to the old custom of placing a sprig of the plant inside a child's cradle. With the protective power of the mistletoe working for them, parents who once feared that their children might be stolen by fairies and replaced with changelings could rest easier at night.

In England it was once believed that if a young woman failed to be kissed beneath a sprig of yuletide mistletoe before her wedding day, she would be forever unable to bear children. Likewise, unable to father children would be the fate of any man who never kissed beneath the yuletide mistletoe while in his bachelorhood.

Many people continue to cling to the old belief that cutting down any mistletoe-bearing tree is a most unlucky thing to do. Some individuals who have done so are said to have met with a violent death as a result. But whether such strange and deadly occurrences are actually the effects of an ancient Druid curse at work or merely odd coincidences, we may never know for sure.

"Too superstitious…is their conceit…that it [mistletoe] hath power against witchcraft, and the illusion of Sathan [Satan], and for that purpose, use to hang a piece thereof at their children's neckes."
—J. Parkinson, *Theatrum Botanicum*, 1640.

Molukka Bean

The Molukka bean (or nut) is a variety of nut native to the Molukka Islands, and popular as an amulet in the Western Isles of Scotland (where they often wash ashore). When worn about the neck, a white Molukka bean is said to turn black to indicate the presence of a sorcerer or a person possessing the evil eye. Some people believe that Molukka beans guard against death in childbirth and drowning.

Moonwort

In the Middle Ages, it was popularly believed among the peasantry of Europe that the fern known as moonwort possessed the power to open or break locks, loosen iron nails, and unshoe horses that tread upon it. An even more curious superstition surrounding the moonwort holds that woodpeckers can acquire the strength to pierce iron if they rub their beaks upon a leaf of this plant. How this bizarre belief entered into the annals of herblore is a mystery.

Mugwort

Sacred to the Pagan goddesses Artemis and Diana, the mugwort is a significant magickal herb and one with many connections to occult folklore.

According to an ancient tradition, a mugwort plant must be picked on the eve of a Summer Solstice in order for its magickal properties to be properly activated. Christians in the Middle Ages seldom pulled a mugwort from the soil of the earth without first making the sign of the cross to ward off any evil spirits that might have taken up residence within the plant.

A small "coal" (said to be actually "old acid roots") found in the ground beneath the roots of a mugwort plant is reputed to be one of the most powerful of all natural amulets. However, occult tradition holds that unless the mugwort plant is uprooted at noon or midnight on St. John's Eve, the "coal" found beneath it shall be without amuletic value.

For those lucky enough to unearth such a treasure, a mugwort's "coal" will offer protection against all "venomous beasts," ward off evil and sorcery, heal all ills (including madness and the plague), inspire feelings of lust in the frigid, bring fertility to those cursed with barrenness, and induce prophetic dreams (especially pertaining to future marriage partners) when placed under a pillow at bedtime.

> *"If they would drink nettles in March,*
> *And eat muggons* [mugwort] *in May,*
> *So many fine maidens*
> *Would go not to the clay."*
> —An old Scottish rhyme.

Peas

It is a good luck sign to find a peapod containing nine peas, and an even luckier one to come across one containing a single pea. If you make a wish while throwing a pod of nine peas over your right shoulder, the chances are good that your wish will come true (but only if you do not repeat it to anyone). It was once believed that a wart could be cured by rubbing it with a pod of nine peas while reciting a special incantation.

Seeds

It was once believed that to accidentally leave any earth unsown in a field brought upon a death in the family before the end of the year, or, depending on the local legend, before the crop is reaped. An old Scottish farming superstition holds that if the weather prevents the sowing of seed after a farmer has taken it out to the field, this is a grim omen.

Shrew-Ash

Centuries ago, it was common in rural England for a live shrew-mouse to be imprisoned within the split trunk of an ash tree and left there to suffocate or starve to death, thus giving the tree incredible magickal powers. Such a tree was known as a "shrew-ash" and its branches and leaves were believed to possess the miraculous powers to heal both man and beast of a wide variety of ailments, including shrew bites.

Willow

In some parts of England it is still believed that willow wood should never be burned on Bonfire Night. To do so invites bad luck. Driving a horse with a stick of willow brings on a stomach ache, while swatting a child or animal with one stunts their growth.

Willow trees have long been valued for their natural ability to protect against sorcery and the evil eye, and some individuals believe that touching them ensures good luck. However, never reveal a secret beneath a willow, otherwise your secrets will be repeated by the wind.

Wood Betony

According to Penelope Ody in *The Complete Medicinal Herbal*, wood betony was the most important herb among the Anglo-Saxons, who found at least 29 medicinal uses for it. She also suggests that wood betony was "possibly the most popular amulet herb, used well into the Middle Ages to ward off evil or ill humors." A ninth century Saxon work called *Herbarium Apuleii* says that wood betony "is good whether for a man's soul or his body; it shields him against visions and dreams." Other popular herbs in Saxon times were mugwort, plantain, vervain, and yarrow, which were used in numerous internal remedies, but most commonly employed as an amulet.

Chapter 3:
Herbal Divination

The art and practice of divination by herbs is one of the oldest methods of prognostication known to mankind. Its formal name is botanomancy, which is derived from the Greek word *botane*, meaning "herb."

Phyllomancy is a type of divination closely related to botanomancy. Diviners who employ this method typically interpret the patterns of veins on leaves to gain insight to future events or to reveal things of the unknown.

Causimomancy is another variation of botanomancy. It draws omens from the ashes produced by the burning of plants and trees. Deriving its name from the Greek word *kaustos* (meaning "burned"), this method of divination also draws omens from the rate at which a plant placed in a fire burns. Traditionally, if a plant smoldered and burned slowly or failed to burn altogether, this was taken as a bad omen. But if it burned rapidly, the omen was good.

Causimomancy has several variants, including capnomancy (the drawing of omens from the various patterns of smoke generated by the burning of flammable botanical material), crithomancy (the interpretation of grain and flour), daphnomancy (the drawing of omens from the smoke and sounds produced by burning laurel wood or leaves), and libanomancy (the divinatory interpretation of incense smoke).

The art and practice of capnomancy is said to have originated in the mysterious land of Babylonia, where it was carried out at certain times of the year when the positions of the planets were most favorable for prognostication. Cedar branches or shavings would be placed upon hot coals or cast into a fire and then priests skilled in the reading of omens would carefully interpret their smoke.

The Druids were said to have believed in and worshipped the spirits of trees and plants, particularly the oak, vervain, and mistletoe. Herbal divination (in addition to rune casting, geomancy, animal prognostication, and other methods) was a practice at which they were highly adept, and many of their divinatory rites were held within the sacred space of oak groves.

The type of herbal divination most commonly employed by the priestly caste of the ancient Celts was a form of capnomancy known as dendromancy. It called for oak branches or mistletoe plants to be ritually cut with a golden sickle and then cast into a blazing fire or set upon live coals. The color and direction of the smoke generated by the burning plant would then be carefully interpreted.

Typically, smoke that rose straight up to the heavens was interpreted as being a favorable omen for the tribe. However, smoke that hung close to the altar was seen as not so favorable. And if it touched the earth, this was believed to be a warning from the spirits or the gods that a new direction or course of action be taken at once.

The early Romans and Greeks, who utilized the divinatory methods of daphnomancy and phyllorhodomancy, respectively, also practiced herbal divination. The art and practice of daphnomancy is believed to have been devised by the augurs of pre-Christian Rome and connected to a sacred grove of laurel trees planted there by various Roman emperors. In the year 68 A.D., the entire grove mysteriously withered and died, as if to portend the death of the Emperor Nero and the demise of the long line of Caesars, which occurred shortly after during that same year. Daphnomancy takes its name from the fabled Greek nymph Daphne, whom the gods changed into a laurel tree.

Libanomancy is a divinatory practice that can be traced back to the magicians of ancient Babylonia. According to the *Three Collated Libanomancy Texts* (translated by Irving L. Finkel), if when you sprinkle incense upon a fire and its smoke drifts to the right, this is an indication that you will prevail over your adversary. However, if the incense smoke drifts to the left, this means that your adversary will prevail over you. If incense smoke clusters, this is a favorable omen of success and financial gain. But if it is fragmented, a financial loss is portended. Beware of incense smoke that "gathers like a date-palm and is thin at its base," for this is a sign of hard times to come. If the rising smoke of incense is cleft (in two), this is said to foretell a loss of one's sanity.

In Greece, divination by observing the leaves and petals of roses (phyllorhodomancy) was a popular method of foretelling future events. *Rosa gallica* (more commonly known in modern times as autumn damask) is believed by many occult historians to have been the flower of choice among the diviners of ancient Greece.

A rose petal with a concave form would first be selected, a yes-or-no question asked, and then a state of meditation entered into. Afterwards, the diviner would place the rose petal in the palm of his or her right hand and then firmly clap both hands together one time. If the petal burst, this indicated an affirmative answer. But if it failed to burst, this was interpreted as a negative reply.

Forecasting the future or gaining answers to questions by interpreting the various sounds produced by the rose petal during the clapping of one's hands is but one of the many variations of phyllorhodomancy.

Herbal divination continues to be practiced in our modern day and age, and in a variety of ways. The plucking of a daisy's petals to determine the true feelings of one's beloved, the picking of a four-leaf clover to attain good luck or to make a wish come true, and counting the number of breaths needed to blow all the fuzzy seeds off a dandelion's stalk to determine how many years will pass before one's wedding day arrives, are all examples of botanomancy in its simplest (and most popular) forms.

Cherry Tree Divination

If you desire to know the number of years you will live, perform the following divination on Midsummer Eve: Run three times clockwise around a cherry tree full of ripe fruit and then shake the tree with all your might as you repeat the following charm:

Cherry tree, I shaketh thee,
Cherry tree, pray tell thou me
How many years am I to live?
By fallen fruit thy answer give.

At the precise moment that you utter the last word of the rhyme, remove your hands from the tree. Count the number of cherries that have fallen to the ground while shaking the tree, and they will reveal to you what age you will live to be. Some diviners interpret the number of fallen cherries as an indication of how many more years one has to live.

Divination to Determine Number of Children

To discover the total number of children you will have in your lifetime, perform this old Scottish method of divination: Go alone into a field of oats at the witching hour on Halloween. With your eyes tightly closed or your vision obscured by a blindfold, spin yourself three times around in a clockwise fashion and then reach out and randomly pull three stalks of oats. After doing this, open your eyes and count the number of grains there are upon the third stalk. This will tell you the number of children that you will father or give birth to.

According to W. Grant Stewart's 19th-century book, *Highlanders of Scotland*, "It may be observed, that it is essential to a female's good name that her stalk should have the top-grain attached to it." Should the top of the stalk be missing, this is taken as a sign that the woman will lose her virginity prior to her wedding day.

Acorn Divination

If you desire to know what fate has in store for you and your fiancée, perform the following divination on a night of the full moon: Take two acorns and mark your initials upon one, and your fiancée's initials upon the other. Place the acorns three inches apart from each other in a cauldron filled with water and then carefully observe their movements.

If they drift towards each other, this is a sure sign that a wedding is in the offing. However, if they drift away from each other, this indicates that you and your fiancée shall part company before your wedding bells ring. If the acorns remain stationary, repeat the divination again at a later time.

Ribwort Marriage Divination

On the eve of Johnsmas (June 25th) or when the moon is full, uproot a ribwort and then place it beneath a flat stone. Allow it to remain there all night, and then carefully examine the root in the morning. If you are destined to wed within the next 12 months, the initials of your future husband or wife will be found upon the plant's root. In England, where many of the love and marriage divinations used by modern Witches and diviners originated, it is traditional for females to divine using the dark variety of the plant, and males with the light.

Sage Marriage Divination

At the witching hour on Halloween, go alone into a garden and, without uttering a single word, pick 12 sage leaves—one at each stroke of the clock. As you pick the 12th leaf at the 12th stroke, the face of your future husband will materialize before you.

If a man's face does not appear to you, this indicates that you will not marry within the next 12 months. (Do not repeat this divination until the following Halloween; otherwise you will invite bad luck!) If a vision of a coffin should appear to you while you are performing this divination, this is said to be an omen of an early death.

Bay Leaf Divinations for Lovers

The following method of divination, when performed on Saint John's Eve, is designed to determine whether or not your lover has been faithful to you: Just before bedtime, take a bay leaf and prick your lover's name or initials upon it with a pin. After doing this, pin the leaf to your brassiere or nightgown so that it will be in place over your heart as you sleep. When you wake up, check the leaf to see if it has turned brown. If it has, this is a sure sign that your beloved has been true to you. But if the leaf is the same color as it was the night before, this is an sign that your lover has (or soon will) deceive you.

To find out if your sweetheart will marry you, prick his or her name or initials upon a bay leaf. Place the leaf inside your left shoe and wear it throughout the day. Allow the leaf to remain in the shoe overnight, and then observe the leaf in the morning. If the name or initials have become darker, this is a sign that your sweetheart will marry you. But if they have grown fainter (or have vanished), this indicates that he or she will not.

To experience a prophetic dream in which the identity of your future husband or wife is revealed to you, pin a bay leaf to your pillow on the eve of Saint Valentine's Day just before going to bed.

The following is a Saint Valentine's Eve love divination from the 18th century work, *Aristotle's Last Legacy*: "Take two Bay-leaves, sprinkle them with Rose-water; the Evening of this day, lay them a cross under your Pillow when you go to bed, putting on a clean Shift and turning it wrong side outwards; and lying down, say: '*Good Valentine be kind to me, In dreams let me my true Love see.*' So crossing your Legs, and go to sleep…you will see in a Dream the Party you are to Marry."

Apple Peel Divination

To determine the first letter of your future spouse's last name, peel an apple in one unbroken strip. By the light of an enchanted pink candle, take the paring in your right hand and recite the following charm three times:

Spirits all-knowing,
May thee reveal
My true love's initials
By shape of this peel.

Turn around thrice and then cast the paring over your left shoulder. If it falls in the shape of an alphabetical letter, this will indicate the initial of your future husband or wife's surname. However, if the apple peel should break upon hitting the floor or ground, this portends that you will never wed.

Clover Divination

Pick a two-leaved clover and place it inside your right shoe. If you are a woman, the first young man you encounter will possess the same first name or initials as the man destined to be your future husband. If you are a man, the first name or initials of your future bride will be revealed by the name of the first young lady you encounter.

Divination by Dreams

If an unmarried woman wishes to dream about the man destined to be her future husband, let her sleep with any of the following herbs beneath her pillow: nine ivy leaves; a sprig of mistletoe taken from a church; or a sprig of myrtle that she has worn in her bosom throughout the day.

Holly Dream Divination

To have a dream about the man or woman destined to be your future husband or wife, perform the following divination on a Friday at the witching hour: Without speaking a single word and taking great care not to be seen, go into a garden and pluck nine leaves from a female (smooth-edged) holly plant. After doing this, knot each leaf into a three-cornered handkerchief. Return home and place the handkerchief beneath your pillow before laying yourself down to sleep.

Myrtle Marriage Divination

If a young woman wishes to find out whether or not her sweetheart will marry her, according to Sidney Oldall Addy's

Household Tales, the following divination should be performed on the Eve of the Summer Solstice (Midsummer Eve): "Let a girl take a sprig of myrtle and lay it in her Prayer Book upon the words of the marriage service, 'Wilt thou have this man to be thy wedded husband?' Then let her close the book, put it under her pillow, and sleep upon it." If the sprig of myrtle is nowhere to be found when she wakes the following morning and opens the book, this is said to be a sure sign that she and her sweetheart will soon be joined together in holy matrimony.

Yarrow Love Divinations

To experience a dream about the man or woman destined to be your future marriage mate, pluck 10 stalks of yarrow on Beltane Eve (April 30th), or on a night when the moon is new. Before going to bed, place nine of the stalks beneath your pillow and toss the remaining one over your left shoulder while repeating the following charm:

> *Good night, good night, fair yarrow,*
> *Thrice good night to thee.*
> *I pray before the dawn tomorrow*
> *My true love to see.*

A similar divinatory method from centuries gone by called for an ounce of yarrow to be sewn up in a piece of flannel or stuffed into a stocking and then placed beneath one's pillow before going to bed. The following spoken charm (or one of its many variations) would then be recited three times:

> *"Thou pretty herb of Venus' tree,*
> *Thy true name it is yarrow.*
> *Now who my future love must be,*
> *Pray tell thou me tomorrow."*

A rather unusual yarrow love divination practiced in England in the Middle Ages instructed young ladies and gentlemen alike to insert a serrated leaf of the yarrow plant into each of their nostrils while reciting a spoken charm. If a nosebleed resulted upon blowing the nose, this was taken as a sure sign that the affections of one's sweetheart were true. However, if the nose did not bleed, this indicated that the love was false.

Rose Dream Divination

Perform the following divination on Midsummer Eve, when the clock chimes 12 to usher in the witching hour: Without uttering a single word, walk backwards into a garden and gather the reddest rose in full bloom. Wrap it in a clean sheet of white paper, and then tuck it away in some secret hiding place where it will be undisturbed.

At sunrise on the day of the old Winter Solstice (December 25th), remove the rose from the paper and place the flower on your bosom. According to legend, the man who is destined to become your husband will then come and snatch it away.

Saint Agnes' Day Divination

Aristotle's Last Legacy (first published in the year 1711) contains a rather interesting divinatory ritual to enable a man or woman to dream about his or her future marriage mate: On Saint Agnes' Day (a time long associated with love divinations and amatory enchantments), take one sprig each of rosemary and thyme, and "sprinkle them with urine thrice." Put one sprig in your left shoe and the other in your right (it matters not which sprig goes in which shoe), and then place your shoes on each side of your bed's head. As you lay yourself down to sleep, recite thrice the following incantation:

> *"Saint Agnes that's to lovers kind,*
> *Come ease the trouble of my mind."*

Hemp Seed Divination

To determine whom their future husbands will be, many young women throughout Europe have used the seeds of the hemp plant in a divinatory ritual that is centuries old. Traditionally performed at the witching hour on either Midsummer Eve or Christmas Eve, hemp divinations (if worked correctly) are said to make the image of one's future husband manifest.

One such method calls for an unmarried girl to walk alone through a garden, field, or churchyard while tossing hemp seeds over her right shoulder and nine times reciting the following magickal rhyme:

> *"Hemp seed I sow,*
> *And hemp seed I hoe,*
> *And he to be my one true love,*
> *Come follow me, I trow."*

A similar version of the hemp seed rhyme is as follows:

> *"I sow hemp seed,*
> *Hemp seed I sow,*
> *He that is to be my husband,*
> *Come after me and mow,*
> *Not in his best or Sunday array,*
> *But in the clothes he wears every day."*

After repeating the rhyme for the ninth time, the girl is then supposed to see a materialization of her husband-to-be standing behind her with a scythe, looking "as substantial as a brass image of Saturn on an old time-piece," according to William Hone's *The Year Book* (1831). However, she must look at him over her left shoulder, otherwise his image will not be visible to her.

Should the girl be destined for a life of spinsterhood (or at least for the next 12 months, according to some traditions), she will not see the image of a man behind her. Instead, she is likely to hear the sound of a bell either chiming softly or ringing loudly.

In the rare event that she should gaze over her left shoulder and see a coffin, this is said to be an omen of an early death for the girl.

Holly Weather Divination

To determine what sort of winter weather lies ahead, according to an old and popular method of divination from New England, examine the number of berries growing on a holly tree. If there are many, this is a sign that inclement weather is in the offing. But if there are few or none, this indicates that the weather will be mild.

Chapter 4:
Tasseography

Tasseography (or tasseomancy) is the art and practice of divination by the reading of tea leaves. Known in Scotland as "reading the cups," it is a popular method of prognostication among many Gypsy fortunetellers and modern Witches alike.

Tasseography is quite ancient in its origin. First practiced in China, it was eventually introduced to Europe and other parts of the world by nomadic Gypsies, who, in exchange for money, food, or favors, could read the fortune and future in the tea leaves of any woman or man who sought their counsel.

During the 19th century, teacup readings were all the rage throughout England and the United States, which, during that period, was experiencing an influx of Gypsy immigrants.

To interpret the future through tea leaves, you will need any type of loose tea and a white (or light-colored) teacup with a wide brim and no pattern on the inside. Any ordinary cup can be used; however, many diviners have a special cup that is used only for tea leaf readings.

Traditionally, a spoonful of tea leaves is placed in the cup, and, before the hot water is added, the person whose fortune is to be told stirs the dried tea with a finger or a spoon while concentrating on a specific question that he or she would like answered. Boiling water is then poured into the cup. After it has cooled, the querent drinks all but one spoonful of the tea.

He or she then takes the cup in his or her left hand and thrice swirls the leaves in a clockwise direction before quickly turning the cup upside down onto a white napkin resting on top of the saucer. After counting to seven (or sometimes nine, depending on the diviner's personal preferences), the cup is returned to its right side up position. The various patterns formed by the wet tea leaves clinging to the bottom and sides of the cup are then interpreted. Some diviners feel that a reading is not complete unless the tea leaves on the napkin are interpreted as well.

Traditionally, a teacup is read clockwise. According to Eva Shaw's *Divining the Future*, "the handle represents the day of the teacup reading and the cup is divided into a years time, with the side directly across the handle indicating six months into the future."

Most readers feel that the closer the tea leaves are to the brim of the cup, the greater their significance. Tea leaves on the bottom of the cup are believed by some to "spell tragedy," and by others to indicate events of the distant future. In many cases, the clockwise or counterclockwise facing of a tea leaf pattern indicates a particular event about to happen or about to draw to a close, respectively.

Examine the tea leaves carefully for any symbols, pictures, letters and/or numbers that are made, for each one possesses a divinatory meaning. For instance, if the leaves take on the shape of a heart, this indicates future happiness. If two hearts are seen, this is said to be a sure sign that wedding bells will be ringing for you (or someone close to you) in the near future. News of a marriage proposal or a wedding will be forthcoming should the symbol of a church, a wedding ring, or a bride and groom be seen.

A dagger is generally perceived to be a warning of impending danger, while a coffin is said to be an omen of death. A moon represents a change soon to take place in one's life, and a ring a change for the better. (However, some tea leaf readers interpret a circular symbol to mean failure!)

Animal symbols are commonly seen in teacup readings. A snake is said to warn against treachery and betrayal. A bird portends good news or perhaps a journey soon to be embarked upon. A dog represents a faithful friend, and a cat a friend who is false.

Dots or dollar signs represent money soon to be received, and a broom traditionally portends a change of residence. A star is always a fortunate sign, and a horseshoe indicates good luck. A triangle or the symbol of a pyramid is one of the best omens to receive. Whenever one appears in a reading, it generally foretells great success.

According to *Welsh Folklore* by J. C. Davies, a good sign is portended if the tea leaves are scattered evenly around the sides of the cup, but an extremely bad one if "the bottom of the cup appears very black with leaves."

The meanings that lie behind the designs and shapes created by the tea leaves can be highly symbolic in their nature, or they can be exactly as they appear. Symbols may hold different meanings for different people; therefore, as with all other methods of divination, the success of a reading rests heavily upon how finely tuned the intuitive powers are of the person conducting the reading.

If you are new to the art and practice of tasseography, do not despair if your first few attempts at reading the tea leaves are unsuccessful. Many readers see only vague shapes in the beginning. But, as the old saying goes, "practice makes perfect." This applies to all skills, including magickal and metaphysical ones as well.

A list of tea leaf symbols and their meanings can be found in the books *Divining the Future* by Eva Shaw (Facts on File, 1995) and *Tea Leaf Reading Symbols* by Harriet Mercedes McCrite (McCrite, 1991).

Tea Spells and Superstitions

In addition to its role in divination, the tea plant (*Camellia* spp.) has long been linked to folk magick and superstition. Burned by Chinese sorcerers to attain wealth, the leaves of the tea plant are often added to money-attracting potions and sachets. Various parts of the tea plant are also used in spells for increasing one's courage and strength, and some modern Witches have been known to use infusions of tea as a base for mixing drinks designed to provoke lust.

A magickal method to keep evil spirits from invading a house or barn calls for tea leaves to be sprinkled upon the ground in front of the building's main entrance. This old Pagan custom is said to be still practiced in some parts of the English Midlands.

Numerous superstitions surround the brewing of tea. For instance, the accidental spilling of tea while it is being made is said to indicate good luck for the mother of the house. However, brewing tea in any teapot other than your own invites bad luck, while forgetting to put in the tea indicates that misfortune is on the horizon. To accidentally make the tea too strong means that you will make a new friend. But to accidentally make it too weak means that you will end up losing one. In England, where the drinking of tea is a national pastime, it is still believed that the arrival of a stranger is portended whenever someone accidentally leaves the lid off his or her teapot.

Take care to always put your sugar into your tea before adding the milk or cream, otherwise you will find yourself quarreling with your husband or wife before the day is done. However, in some parts of England it was once believed that if a young girl added milk or cream to her tea before putting in the sugar, she would never wed.

It is extremely unlucky for two people to pour out of the same teapot, according to an old superstition, which can be found alive and well in many parts of the world. And never pour tea with another person unless you wish to become a magnet for bad luck.

Bubbles or a circle of foam on the surface of a cup filled with tea is said to be a sign that money will soon be received. Some folks believe that money is indicated only if the bubbles or foam appear in the center of the cup. If they appear near the sides, this is a sign that you will soon be kissed!

If a piece of tea stem (known as a "stranger") should float to the top of your cup of tea, this is said to be a sign that a visitor will arrive. If the stem is hard, this indicates that the visitor will be a man. If it is tender, the visitor will be a woman.

To determine which day of the week your visitor will come to call, place the stem on the back of your left hand and then slap it with the palm of your other hand. Each time you do this, recite one of the days of the week (starting with the current day). The day of the week that is recited when the stem either sticks to the palm of your right hand or falls off indicates which day it will be.

A similar divination method, which was popular in Victorian-era England, was carried out to determine the fidelity of one's lover. A wet tea stalk or long tea leaf would be placed in the palm of the right hand, and then both hands would be clapped together once. If the tea stalk or leaf remained stuck to the palm of the right hand after being clapped, this indicated a faithful lover. However, if it adhered to the other palm, this indicated one who was fickle.

To avoid bad luck, always be sure to stir your tea in a clockwise direction, and never stir the leaves in a teapot prior to pouring. To stir your tea with a fork, a knife, or anything other than a spoon is to invite bad luck. And never stir another person's tea, for to do so will stir up strife.

In addition to the numerous good and bad luck omens associated with tea, there are many tea-based superstitions concerning human fertility. For example, if a man and a woman pour a cup of tea from the same teapot, they will end up having a child together. If a young lady permits a man to pour her more than one cup of tea, she will be unable to resist his sexual charms. A woman who pours tea in another woman's house will soon find herself pregnant (or, according to another superstition, the recipient of very bad luck). Some folks believe that if two women should take hold of the same teapot at once, this will cause one of them to give birth to red-haired twins before the year reaches its end! And if more than one person pours you a cup of tea, this is also believed to result in the birth of twins (though not necessarily red-haired).

Regardless whether your tea leaves are used in the casting of a spell, the divining of the future, or simply the brewing of a cup of hot tea, you should never throw them away after you are finished using them. To do so is said to bring bad luck, according to some superstitious folks. Disposing of your used tea leaves by casting them into a fire not only prevents bad luck, but keeps poverty away.

Spell For Using Mugwort Tea

by Lee Prosser

Mugwort is used to conjure visions, pursue dream quests, open the partaker up to the inner planes for astral travel, and to see into the future.

Prepare mugwort for tea, and then address the goddesses Bast and Durga in the following manner as the tea brews:

Bless this tea in the names
of Bast and Durga
that the goddesses grant
it vision and strength
for my mind.

Prior to drinking the tea, address the goddesses Bast and Durga in the following manner:

Beloved Bast, Beloved Durga,
Beloved Durga, Beloved Bast,
Bless my mugwort tea
with that which I need to
restore myself
so that I may once again
be made whole.
Thank you Bast, thank you Durga,
So mote it be,
So will it be,
So it is done.

Chapter 5: Healing by Root & Flower

Lee Prosser is a dear friend of mine who was born and raised in Southwest Missouri, where the old ways of the hill people and the mysteries of that area left positive impressions on his life.

According to Lee, "There is no heaven, no hell, only continuity. And what is done prior to that is always helped along with a good cup of herbal tea." An interesting statement, and one that I (being the tea lover that I am) am inclined to agree with.

In the following paragraphs, Lee discusses four of his favorite herbal teas and some of their unusual properties:

"Mullein (*Verbascum thapsus*), also known as Aaron's rod, foxglove, velvet plant, shepherd's club, candlewick plant, flannel flower, lungwort, and feltwort, grows wild in the United States. To herbalists, it acts as an astringent, emollient, pectoral, and demulcent. For the lungs, it has an invigorating effect, and can be used for sore throats. To make mullein tea, gently bruise one mullein leaf, pick into small pieces, and drop into one cup of cold water. Bring to a boil, and then allow it to cool before drinking. Use a strainer to remove the leaf pieces as the tea is poured into a cup. (Note: A nice two-inch square leaf will make one cup of tea.) In India, mullein is thought to possess great properties of protection against evil when carried in a small pouch on the person, or hung in the home. Kept under the pillow, it safeguards the sleeper from nightmares. Some say a leaf of mullein can be carried on the person to attract love from the opposite sex! Personally, I like the taste of mullein tea on a cool winter night in front of a glowing, warm fireplace. My cat Roz likes to sip the tea also.

"Mugwort (*Artemisia vulgaris*), also known as St. John's plant, grows wild in the United States. Mugwort is well known as a tonic, but it is also a stimulant, a nervine, an emmenagogue, and a diaphoretic. To make mugwort tea, take a leaf of the plant and follow the same instructions as given above for mullein tea. Drink before beginning divinations and seeking prophetic dreams. Old beliefs suggest that it has the power to protect from evil if carried on the person, safeguarding one from many forms of harm. Perhaps its greatest gift is that it aids in astral projection. For this, some suggest drinking a cup of mugwort tea prior to bedtime, placing some mugwort under you pillow, and rubbing a leaf around your nose area. Mugwort is an unusual herb. I call it the opener of the gate to other worlds.

"Dandelion (*Taraxacum officinale*), also known as lion's tooth, puffball, blowball, and white endive, grows wild in the United States. It is best known for its role as a stimulant and a tonic. Its leaves are used as greens in salads, and its roasted roots (ground-up and prepared in the same way as coffee) have a stimulating effect on the body. Served hot or cold, dandelion tea has a remarkable taste. Some of its properties include the calling of spirits, developing psychic abilities, and foreseeing the future.

"Peppermint (*Mentha piperita*), also known as balm mint, grows wild in the United States. It is best known for its role as a stimulant, antispasmodic, and carminative. It is believed to aid in helping the heart and aiding indigestion. Take a leaf and prepare in the same manner as explained in making mullein tea. I have always liked all of the mint teas, but prefer peppermint best of all. Its properties include purification spells, healing spells, and happiness spells. If leaves are rubbed upon household items and corners of home walls, protection from evil forces is achieved, which has been an old belief concerning the power of the peppermint leaf! Many sources say it can be a direct aid in astral travel. Perhaps combining it with mugwort would give an added boost to astral travels! Some claim that peppermint increases psychic powers. Peppermint leaf is also picked fresh and chewed raw.

"Herbal tea seeks out the person it needs to be with at a given time and place, and it will fulfill that person's needs. Listen to what the tea says to you. Let your intuition blend with the vision of the tea you are drinking, and experience the herbal healing that is yours for the asking."

A Wortcunning Rhyme

Seeds and deeds,
Be sown on days
In harmony with lunar phase.
Quick or slow,
They sprout and grow
And soon turn into grand bouquets.
Leaf and flower,
Root and thorn,
Harvest on a Solstice morn.
Then the powers that you seek
Shall be firmly at their peak.

—*from* Priestess and Pentacle
by Gerina Dunwich

To Ward Off Illnesses and Wounds

Wear or carry a mojo bag stuffed with one or more of the following herbs: angelica, cowslip flowers, garlic cloves, a ginseng root, mugwort, rosemary, rowan berries and/or bark, rue leaves, vervain, willow leaves and/or bark, or yerba santa leaves.

The Bramble Bush Spell

Long ago it was believed that if an ill person crawled backward and then forward three times under the natural arch formed by a bramble bush (a blackberry) rooted at both ends, he or she would be made well. This simple magickal method supposedly worked to cure a variety of ailments, such as boils, rheumatism, and even blackheads.

"Thrice under a Bryer doth creepe, which at both ends was rooted deepe…Her magicke much availing."—Michael Drayton. *Nymphidia*, 1751.

In the Middle Ages, horses that were said to have been "shrew-runne" (paralyzed by the bite of a shrew) would often be drawn through a bramble arch to be magickally cured of the afflictions.

To cure a child suffering from whooping cough, let him or her be passed nine times under and nine times over a bramble arch while the following incantation is recited:

Under the bramble and over the bramble,
I wish to leave the chin-cough here!

Repeat this spell for three mornings in a row, just before the rising of the sun and while facing East.

The Christianized version of this spell called for the Lord's Prayer to be recited while the afflicted person was passed under the bramble arch. In addition, the patient was required to eat a bit of buttered bread, and then feed the rest of the loaf to a wild bird or animal. The eating of the bread was believed to transfer the illness from the person to the poor unfortunate creature, which would soon die.

To Guard Against Hepatitis

An old spell once used by Witches to ward off hepatitis calls for 13 garlic cloves to be strung together on a white cord and then worn around the neck for 13 consecutive days and nights.

At the witching hour of midnight on the last night, go to a deserted crossroads. Take off the garlic necklace and toss it over your right shoulder while looking straight ahead. Upon doing this, return home as quickly as possible and take care not to look back lest the spell be made broken.

Respiratory Tract Infections

To help treat respiratory tract infections such as bronchitis and pleurisy, place one teaspoon of shredded elecampane in a saucepan. Add one cup of cold water, then gently simmer for fifteen minutes. Allow the brew to cool before drinking. Take up to three cups per day.

If you are new to the taste of elecampane, be warned that it is an extremely bitter herb! To counter its unpleasant taste, you may find it helpful to add a spoonful or two of honey to the brew. Also take care not to consume elecampane in large amounts as it can be quite upsetting to the system.

A soothing homemade chest rub can easily be made by mixing ten drops of thyme essential oil into one teaspoon of almond oil. When rubbed upon the chest, it works well to help break up and get rid of the infected phlegm and congestion that accompanies acute and chronic bronchitis.

To Guard Against Rheumatism

To guard against rheumatism, many Witches of the past performed the following herbal spells:

Take an elder twig and knot it thrice. Enchant it by visualization and spoken spell, and then carry it in your pocket. Elder has long been held to be an effective charm against rheumatism.

A pocketful of nutmeg or horse chestnut (also known as buckeye) is also believed to do the trick!

Another simple herbal spell to guard against rheumatism calls for the leaves of a goat's rue plant to be gathered at dawn on the day of the Summer Solstice and then placed inside one's shoes prior to putting them on.

Practitioners of folk magick have long used the potato to cure, as well as to prevent, a variety of illnesses. Carry in your pocket a potato inscribed with a pentagram to protect yourself against rheumatism, warts, gout, toothaches, and the common cold.

Herbs to Treat Morning Sickness

To alleviate the symptoms of nausea and vomiting associated with morning sickness, chew and swallow a few aniseeds and/or inhale the scent of crushed fresh peppermint leaves or peppermint essential oil. **Warning: Do not take peppermint oil internally. It can be quite toxic, even in small quantities. Peppermint tea, which contains volatile oils that may over stimulate the nervous system of an unborn child, should also be avoided by pregnant women.**

For severe morning sickness, steep one teaspoon of grated gingerroot (or a one-inch-long chunk of peeled gingerroot), ½ teaspoon of spearmint, and ½ teaspoon of meadowsweet in one cup of boiling water for 10 to 20 minutes. Strain and sweeten with honey or sugar (if desired) before drinking. Many herbalists recommend two to three cups per day. **Warning: Women who have a history of miscarriage should avoid using ginger. When taken internally in large amounts, this herb may bring on miscarriage in the early months of pregnancy.**

White Willow Bark for Arthritis

To relieve the inflammation in sore joints, many Witches and folk healers alike have relied on tea made from the bark of the white willow.

The directions for making this healing (but unpleasant-tasting) tea are as follows: Steep one teaspoon of white willow bark in one cup of boiling water, covered, for 15 minutes. Strain and sweeten with a bit of honey or sugar (if desired) before drinking.

For best results, drink one cup in the morning, one in the afternoon, and one in the evening.

To Ward Off Arthritis

An old hoodoo method to ward off arthritis calls for the root of a plant known as devil's bone to be cut into small pieces with a silver blade and then put into a charm bag made of red flannel. Wear or carry the charm bag at all times and, according to practitioners, your joints will be free from the pain and stiffness of arthritis.

A Modern Witch's Herbal Cure for Athlete's Foot

When the moon is in a waning phase, puree nine cloves of garlic in an electric blender or food processor. Fill a small tub with enough hot (but not scalding) water to cover your feet. Add the pureed garlic, along with six drops of tea tree oil, and then allow your feet to soak in it for approximately 20 minutes. Repeat once or twice a day until the athlete's foot condition is cleared up.

Caution: To avoid irritation, do not apply garlic directly to your skin. Also be warned that after a good soak in a garlic footbath, your feet will hardly come out smelling like roses! But despite the pungent (but temporary) odor that it leaves on the feet, this natural remedy has been known in many cases to eradicate an athlete's foot problem within a matter of a few days.

To Prevent Seasickness

Throughout the coastal regions of New England, it was once believed that pennyroyal flowers carried on board a ship could be used as a charm to prevent attacks of seasickness from occurring.

The eating of lettuce leaves prior to a seafaring journey was also reputed to be highly effective in combating seasickness. However, some folks believed that this spell only worked if the lettuce was picked from a Witch's garden at the stroke of midnight, and on a night when the moon was positioned in one of the three water signs of the zodiac.

Wart Charming

Three old herbal spells to cure warts are as follows:

Spell 1: When the moon is on the wane, rub the wart with a dried bean. As you do this, recite the following incantation 13 times:

> *Bean to wart, and wart to bean,*
> *I enchant thee times thirteen.*
> *As the earth brings your decay*
> *So shall this wart be charmed away!*

Without speaking a word, dig a small hole in the ground and place the bean within it. Fill in the hole with soil, and then spit upon it 13 times to seal the spell. As the buried bean decays, so shall the wart grow smaller and smaller until it is finally no more.

Spell 2: When the moon is in a waning phase, rub the wart with a twig cut from an elder tree with a blade of silver. As you do this, visualize the wart being magickally transferred from your body into the twig. At the midnight hour, bury the elder twig in some mud and leave it there to rot.

Spell 3: Seven days after the moon has been at her fullest, rub the wart with the cut edge of an onion. As you do this, recite the following incantation while visualizing the wart being magickally absorbed into the onion:

Into this onion, wart be carried;
In the Mother Earth be buried.
As the soil brings your decay,
So shall this wart be charmed away!

Go to a deserted crossroads and, as the first bell of the witching hour tolls, toss the onion over your right shoulder without uttering a single word. Return home, as quickly as possible and without looking back, otherwise the spell shall be rendered impotent.

To Cure a Boil

To rid yourself of a boil according to Pliny's *Natural History*, take nine grains of barley and trace a circle around the boil thrice with each grain. After doing this, cast the grains of barley into a fire using your left hand.

To Cure a Sty

An old and simple spell from the leprechaun-enchanted land of Ireland calls for a gold wedding ring and a thorn from a gooseberry bush.

When the moon is on the wane (and only during this lunar phase), touch or prick the sty with the thorn inserted through the ring. Do this nine times, each time shouting the word, "away!" This is reputed to make the sty vanish quickly and never return.

Other magickal sty-curing methods from centuries past (similar to those used for charming away warts) included rubbing the sty with a twig cut from an elder tree and then burying the twig, and rubbing a bean pod nine times upon the sty, then burying it under an ash tree. But in order for either spell to be effective, they had to be carried out in secret and on a night when the moon was waning.

Chapter 6:
Herbs of the
Ancient Sorcerers

*"Sorcery! We are all sorcerers, and live in
a wonderland of marvel and beauty
if we did but know it"* —Charles Godfrey Leland

Belladonna

Belladonna was a poisonous plant prized by sorcerers of centuries past, who used it to induce psychic visions and astral projections. Known by many as "deadly nightshade," belladonna was also a popular ingredient in magickal poisons used by some sorcerers to inflict death or madness upon their enemies and rivals. According to *The Warlock's Book* by Peter Haining, "fourteen of its berries will produce death. Half that number will cause wild excitement and delirium."

Witches of old were said to have used belladonna in their flying ointments and cauldron brews. Although extremely toxic, belladonna was also used in a number of folk cures and even consumed (in very small quantities) by those who desired to see into the future.

Belladonna was also believed by many to keep evil spirits at bay. Sprigs or garlands of the plant were often placed around the home or hung over beds and cradles to protect sleeping adults and children from the evils that lurked in the night. Ironically, belladonna was also used by many farmers to guard their livestock against sorcery, despite its widespread reputation for being one of the spellcasters' most favored banes and the old saying that this plant was tended by the Devil himself.

Hellebore

In ancient times, hellebore was used in many rituals of exorcism. Dried and burned, it was believed to drive out demons from possessed human beings and animals alike, and banish malevolent ghosts from the dwellings and other places in which they took delight haunting.

It is said that sorcerers in the Middle Ages would scatter powdered hellebore on the ground before them as they walked in order to attain invisibility. Many sorcerers and Witches also used the plant to induce astral projections.

Henbane

Known by the folk names "black nightshade," "devil's eye," "Jupiter's bean," and "poison tobacco," the henbane is a poisonous plant that was commonly used by sorcerers of old in rituals to conjure forth demons and "fantastic apparitions." It was also used in the art of weatherworking, as the plant was believed to hold the power to bring forth rain from the heavens above.

Like many of the Old World plants used by practitioners of the Black Arts, henbane was attributed with divinatory powers and employed by those who were masters of the art of prophecy. It was a main ingredient in sorcerer's salves and flying ointments, and many old grimoires indicate that henbane, along with opium and thornapple, were the three banes (poisonous herbs) most favored by devotees of sorcery.

Despite its toxicity, henbane was, at one time, an herb also associated with amatory enchantments. Interestingly, it was believed that a woman could be made to fall in love with a man if he wore or carried henbane in a charm bag. However, in order for the plant to work its magick effectively for the sorcerer, he needed to gather it at dawn. It was also imperative that he did it skyclad (nude) and while standing on one foot, according to the late Scott Cunningham in *Cunningham's Encyclopedia of Magical Herbs.* There is no mention as to why this curious procedure stood on.

Mandrake

The mandrake (*Mandragora officinarum*) is perhaps the most magickal of all plants associated with spell casters of old. This highly toxic plant is potent in all forms of enchantment, from the most tender of love spells to the most evil of curses. It has also been used, among other purposes, to divine the future, gain arcane knowledge, awaken or increase a person's clairvoyant powers, attract good luck, lead its master or mistress to the location of buried or hidden treasure, attract money, promote fertility in barren women, and work (reputedly) as a powerful aphrodisiac.

The part of the mandrake most commonly employed in magickal workings is the plant's curious human-shaped root. In medieval times, they were often dried, powdered, and then added to ointments that were said to endow Witches with the powers of flight and sorcerers with the powers of invisibility.

To properly harness the energies of a mandrake root, according to occult tradition, you must first pull it from the earth on a night when the moon is full. Some magicians claim that a mandrake will work its magick only for the individual who uproots it, thus rendering store-bought roots useless, aside from being collector's items and curiosity pieces. The next step, which is outlined in my book, *Magick Potions*, calls for the mandrake root to rest in your house, undisturbed, for a period of three days. On the third night, the root must be put into a bowl or small cauldron of water and allowed to soak overnight. At sunrise, take the mandrake root from the bowl or cauldron, dry it thoroughly, and then dress it in a piece of silk cloth and do not allow anyone, other than yourself, to touch the root or even gaze upon it. This is basically the same procedure that the sorcerers of old followed in order to activate the mandrake root's mysterious occult powers.

The mandrake is sacred to a number of Pagan deities, including Hecate and Diana, and to the legendary sorceresses, Circe (Greek) and the Alrauna Maiden (Teutonic). Its association with the Black Arts was no doubt responsible for its acquisition of such folk names as the "warlock weed" and the "devil's candle."

"Who may fynde a true mandrake and lay him between a pair of white sheets and present him meat and drink twice a day, notwithstanding then he neither eateth nor drinketh, he that does it shall become rich within short space."

—*Gospelles of Dystaues*, 1507.

Poison Hemlock

As its name implies, the poison hemlock is a highly toxic plant that, under no circumstances, should be eaten or used in potions intended for human consumption. A good number of sorcerers and sorceresses in the Middle Ages are know to have met their fate experimenting with this magickal, but deadly, plant. Hemlock was the poison of choice for Socrates, who died by his own hand after being sentenced to death.

A plant sacred to the Greek goddess Hecate, hemlock is said to have been used by some Witches of old to induce astral projections and also to render men sexually impotent. The extracted juice from the plant was rubbed onto the blades of ritual daggers and swords for purification and magickal empowerment prior to their use.

Wolf's Bane

Wolf's bane (also known as "aconite" and "monkshood") is probably best known for its use as an herbal amulet against vampires and werewolves. However, according to legend, the protective powers of the wolf's bane plant are only effective when its flowers are in full bloom. It is also reputed to have the power to cure those who have fallen victim to the curse of lycanthropy.

To master invisibility, some sorcerers in the Middle Ages were said to have carried with them a magickal charm consisting of a wolf's bane seed wrapped in the skin of a lizard. It is unknown whether or not this charm helped them to return to their visible state, or if simply willing it was the only thing needed to regain their visibility.

The Magickal History of Hemp

Also known by the folk names "gallowgrass," "ganja," and "neckweed," the hemp is an intoxicating plant with a long magickal history. Being a common ingredient in many love spells from centuries gone by, it was also added to love potions to inspire the affections of others. Additionally, it was believed to facilitate the psychic powers, and for this reason it was often dried and burned by diviners as incense (along with mugwort) prior to, and during, the scrying of magick mirrors.

In China, it was once widely believed that demons were responsible for illnesses that plagued mankind. To drive out such demons from an afflicted person, Chinese sorcerers would fashion strands of dried hemp into a scourge that resembled a snake, and then thrash it against the patient's bed while uttering special incantations.

In medieval times, hemp was used as one of the mind-altering herbal ingredients of "sorcerer's grease"—a magickal ointment reputed to be used by sorcerers and sorceresses for flying, shapeshifting, and invisibility.

Chapter 7:
Hoodoo Herbs

The art and practice of hoodoo (which is also known as "conjure," "conjuration," and "root work") is an African-American tradition of folk magick.

The origin of the word "hoodoo" is a mystery. It is known to have been in use in the United States since the 19th century (and probably earlier), and is believed to be African.

Not to be confused with Voodoo (a Haitian religion), hoodoo is neither a religion nor a religious denomination, and is therefore not capitalized. Although it incorporates elements from various religions of Africa and Europe in terms of its core beliefs, hoodoo is not connected to any specific form of theology or religious worship. It is, however, a tradition that emphasizes personal power through various magickal means (such as mojo bags, foot track magick, crossings, and crossroads magick).

Hoodoo is a unique blending of African religious beliefs and customs with Native American herb lore and European folk magick. Practiced by blacks and whites alike, its popularity is strongest throughout the southern regions of the United States.

Hoodoo, like many other traditions of folk magick, attributes magickal properties to herbs and roots. Among the many plants used in hoodoo spells, by far the most popular ones are as follows:

Angelica Root

The root of the angelica is commonly used by hoodoo practitioners for the purposes of warding off evil, uncrossing, breaking jinxes, and attaining good luck (especially in matters concerning one's health or family.) When anointed with three drops of "Peaceful Home Oil" and carried in a blue mojo bag with a pinch of lavender flowers, an angelica root is said to bring peace and tranquility to one's home and protect their marriage against infidelity.

Buckeye Nuts

Buckeye nuts are believed by some hoodoo "doctors" to increase a man's sexual power. Shaped like miniature testicles, they are sometimes carried in the pants pockets as charms to bring men "good fortune in sexual matters." In the southern and eastern regions of the United States, buckeyes are carried in mojo bags to cure or prevent such ailments as arthritis, rheumatism, and migraine headaches.

However, the buckeye is probably best known for its use as a gambler's good luck charm. Traditionally, a hole is drilled into the nut, filled with quicksilver (mercury), and then sealed with wax. For maximum effectiveness, the charm should be prepared on a Wednesday during a planetary hour of Mercury, the reason for this being that the god to whom this day and hour correspond is one who governs games of chance and sleight of hand. Some gamblers carry their buckeye charms in a mojo bag (often along with a silver "Mercury" dime) and anoint it with any luck-attracting occult oil (such as "Fast Luck") prior to placing their bets.

Devil Pod

The devil pod (also known as "bat nut" and "goat head") is the glossy black seedpod of an aquatic Asian plant, *Trapa bicornis*. Naturally shaped like a flying bat or a goat-horned devil, these unusual pods also have what has been described as

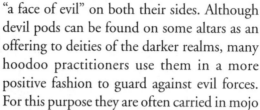

"a face of evil" on both their sides. Although devil pods can be found on some altars as an offering to deities of the darker realms, many hoodoo practitioners use them in a more positive fashion to guard against evil forces. For this purpose they are often carried in mojo bags or positioned above doorways, facing outward like the guardian "door demons" found perched above the entrances to ancient Tibetan temples.

Devil's Shoestring

The root of the devil's shoestring is another powerful hoodoo amulet favored by those with a passion for playing lotteries and betting on games of chance. Carried in a red flannel mojo bag, it draws gambling luck, protects against evil and accidental poisoning, stops others from spreading gossip about you, wards off crossings, and helps one to find and/or maintain employment.

Some hoodoo practitioners believe that devil's shoestring roots need to be kept in a jar filled with whiskey and spirits of camphor when they are not in use.

High John the Conqueror

The root known as High John the Conqueror is one of the staples of hoodoo magick. Legend has it that this root was named after an African king who was sold into slavery but able to outsmart his captors through his cleverness.

High John the Conqueror is popular as a charm to conquer any situation, achieve success in any undertaking, attract money, protect against evil and harm, increase one's strength and/or confidence, gain mastery, ensure good luck (especially involving lotteries and games of chance), break jinxes and hexes, cure depression, and enhance male sexual power. Male practitioners of hoodoo love magick also use it to win the hearts of women.

In the early decades of the 20th century, a spiritual supplies company began production of High John the Conqueror perfume. Containing a piece of root in each bottle, the magickal fragrance was worn mainly by men for attracting the opposite sex as well as increasing their luck at gambling.

The essential oil of High John the Conqueror is used by hoodoo practitioners to dress altar candles and anoint mojo bags. The root is commonly made into sachet powders, incense, and crystals for bath or floor wash. As far as magickal plants are concerned, High John the Conqueror is said to have no equal.

One example of a High John the Conqueror money-drawing mojo is as follows: Take a two-dollar bill bearing a leap year date and wrap it around a High John the Conqueror root and a silver "Mercury" dime (Winged Liberty Head dime issued from 1916 to 1945). Take care to fold the bill towards you, and not away from you. Place it in a green flannel mojo bag and anoint it daily with three drops of High John the Conqueror Oil or any occult oil designed for money-drawing. (Although green is a color believed by many magickal practitioners to possess money-drawing energies, some hoodoo "doctors" prefer to use red flannel for their money-drawing mojos.) Keep the mojo with you at all times (even when you sleep) and you will soon begin to see an increase in your wealth.

Lucky Hand Root

Lucky hand (also known as a "salep root" and a "five-finger root") is a name given to the root of several species of orchids. Resembling a small human hand with three to 10 fingers, this root is among the most powerful ingredients that can be added to a mojo bag for gambling luck, protection against accidents and illnesses, finding and/or maintaining employment, achieving success, and increasing personal power and mastery (especially when combined with five-finger grass and a High John the Conqueror root.) In his herbal encyclopedia, author Scott Cunningham refers to the Lucky Hand as "one of the most famous New Orleans magical botanicals."

A powerful magickal oil made from the lucky hand root is sold in many occult shops and botanicas under the name, lucky hand oil. Many gamblers rub a bit of it on their hands prior to an evening's play in the belief that it will hoodoo the cards or dice in their favor.

Another favorite gambler's trick to increase luck at games of chance and ward off losing streaks is to secretly sprinkle some powdered lucky hand root upon their money before betting it. This simple magickal procedure is known as "marking the money" and many a gambling man (and woman) firmly believe that it keeps Lady Luck at their side.

Chapter 8:
Gypsy Herb Magick

The Gypsies are a nomadic people believed to have originally been "low-caste Hindu exiles" from northern India. Having absorbed the religious and folk customs of the many lands through which their caravans sojourned, the Gypsies came to incorporate elements of both Paganism and Christianity into their practices.

"Gypsies have been renowned practitioners of magical arts, and they have undoubtedly had a profound influence on the development of folk magic," states author Rosemary Ellen Guiley in *The Encyclopedia of Witches and Witchcraft*. There can be no denying that the tradition of these mysterious travelers of the world is abundant with superstitions and bewitchments.

Mother's Gypsy Fertility Charm

Being brought up in a Queens, New York, neighborhood not far from a Romanian Gypsy settlement that existed in Maspeth from the mid-1920s until 1939, my mother was both leery of, and intrigued by, the Gypsies. Like many other children growing up in the early decades of the 20th century, she was frightened by the old stories she heard of Gypsies stealing babies and was warned by her elders that the Gypsies were a people not to be trusted.

This, however, did not prevent her from later marrying a man whose paternal grandfather was a Gypsy from Bohemia. Nor did it stop her in the spring of 1959 from seeking the counsel of a *chovihani* (a Gypsy-Witch) after her two consecutive attempts to have a child resulted in miscarriages.

According to my mother's account, the Gypsy woman first read her palm and then her tea leaves in a cup that was marked all the way around with astrological symbols. After interpreting the signs, she then presented my mother with a small silk pouch that contained a root (which I strongly suspect was from a mandrake plant) and instructed her to keep it with her, day and night, throughout the entire term of her next pregnancy. Desperate to have a child and willing to try just about anything at that point, my mother followed the Gypsy's advice. Two days after Christmas in 1959 as an afternoon snowstorm raged, I finally came screaming and kicking my way into the world. (This, incidentally, is how one of my magickal names, "Lady Mandragora," came to be, although my mother always affectionately referred to me as her "little witchling.")

In 1962 my mother tried a fourth (and final) time to have a child but failed to use the Gypsy's fertility charm as she had done during her previous pregnancy, which led to my birth. In October of that year, while sitting in the living room with my father and watching a television news broadcast about the Cuban missile crisis, my mother suddenly took ill and lost the baby. Coincidence? You decide.

Not surprisingly, Gypsy folk magick and divination have long been two of my passions. An interest in old Gypsy customs developed early on in my life despite the fact that my father never discussed his Gypsy heritage. For whatever reason he had, whether it was a sense of shame instilled during his childhood or a fear of discrimination from the predominantly Irish community in which we lived, he made it a point not to let others know that his ethnic roots encompassed more than just Irish and Czech. In fact, I was not even aware that my paternal grandmother was a Native American hailing from the Hopi Tribe in Arizona until my bereaved grandfather mentioned it at her funeral. Around the age of 10 I found myself drawn to cartomancy (divination by cards), and by my early teen years, I was already experimenting with some of the spells contained in Charles Godfrey Leland's *Gypsy Sorcery and Fortune Telling*.

In Leland's book, the Gypsies of England are said to be believers in Witches existing among their own people. These Witches are feared for their powers, but are not associated with the devil. Leland calls it "remarkable" that the Gypsies regard their Witches as "exceptionally gifted sorcerers or magicians" rather than "special limbs of Satan."

Gypsy folk magick draws heavily upon the use of herbs and other natural amulets, particularly seashells, eggs, animal teeth, and human hair. It also seems that a great deal of Gypsy spells are aimed primarily at the attainment of love and the warding off of the evil eye, the power of which many Gypsies both believe in and fear greatly.

Herbal Amulets for Protection

There are a variety of herbs, and other amulets, used by a Gypsy chovihani for protection. Among the most popular is garlic, which is often placed under a woman in childbirth to keep her, as well as her newborn baby, safe from any onlookers who may possess the evil eye. Garlic is also rubbed upon the spines of horses during the waning of the moon to have them "always in good spirits and lively."

Hungarian Gypsies believe that hanging the twigs from a thistle plant on a stable door will protect horses, as well as other animals, from bewitchment.

The wolf's bane is another plant believed to have great protective powers. Centuries ago, many of the Gypsies in Romania were said to have valued it as an amulet to guard against those with the power to shapeshift into wolves.

Gypsy Love Magick

Rye is a popular herb in Gypsy love magick. When baked into bread and then served to a loved one, rye seeds are believed to secure the affections of that person.

The pimento is another plant associated with Gypsy love magick. The continental Gypsies, according to Scott Cunningham, have used it in their amatory spells and sachets for hundreds of years. When enchanted and secretly put  in the food of another, it supposedly causes that individual to develop deep romantic feelings for him or her.

A love charm popular among the English Gypsies is mentioned in Charles Godfrey Leland's book of *Gypsy Sorcery and Fortune Telling*. It calls for an onion or a tulip bulb to be planted in a clean and previously unused pot, while the name of one's beloved is recited. Every day at both sunrise and sunset, the following incantation should be said over the pot:

"As this root grows
And as this blossom blows,
May his [or her] heart be
Turned unto me!"

As each day passes, "the one whom you love will be more and more inclined to you, till you get your heart's desire."

There is an old belief among Gypsies that willow-knots (willow twigs that have naturally grown into a knot) are twined by fairy-folk, and to undo one invites bad luck. To recover stolen goods, a Gypsy man will often tie a string around a willow-knot and say: "With this string I bind the thief's luck!" But if it is the love of a particular woman that he desires, he will cut the willow-knot and hold it in his mouth while, at the same time, turning his thoughts to the woman and reciting the following spoken charm:

"I eat thy luck,
I drink thy luck,
Give me the luck of thine,
Then thou shall be mine."

To add even more power to the spell, the willow-knot should then be hidden in the desired woman's bed without her knowledge of it.

If a man wishes to make a certain woman fall in love with him, an old Gypsy love spell instructs that he should secretly obtain one of her shoes, fill it with rue leaves, and then hang it over the bed in which he sleeps.

Magickal powers are attributed to the roots of trees, particularly the ash and the alraun, and it is said that many Gypsy-Witches cunning in the art of love enchantment know how to use them in the preparation of love philters (potions).

An old Gypsy recipe to make an aphrodisiac calls for the fresh roots of an asparagus plant to be boiled in red wine. It is said that if any man or woman drinks the wine for seven consecutive mornings (in place of breakfast), he or she will be overcome by lustful urges.

Many Gypsies also believe that beans are powerful aphrodisiacs when eaten, and function as sexual amulets when carried in one's pocket or in a *putsi,* a special silk or chamois pouch or charm bag used by Gypsies in the same manner that a mojo bag is used by a hoodoo "doctor."

A piece of orrisroot carried in a putsi is another common Gypsy love amulet, as is the mysterious human-shaped root of the European mandrake plant. In addition to arousing sexual passions, the mandrake is believed to ensure an everlasting love between a couple when both partners carry with them a piece of root from the same plant.

Fern seeds are also a staple in the art of Gypsy love magick. Men traditionally give love potions brewed from the seeds of a male fern to the women they desire, while women tradition-ally give those brewed from the seeds of a female fern to the men whose hearts they wish to win over.

Vervain is also another plant favored by the Gypsies for the drawing of love, as well as for the attraction of good luck. It is said that vervain must be gathered on the first day of the new moon before sunrise or it will not be magickally effective. Carry its dried flowers in a putsi or place them beneath your pillow before you sleep and, according to Gypsy legend, the love of another you will invite.

Gypsies are well aware of the intense powers that their love spells hold. Many who wish to keep themselves immune from such amatory bewitchments or counteract the magick of any unwelcome love enchantment used upon them have been known to wear over their heart a small putsi made of white silk and filled with seven leaves from the angelica plant.

Earth-Spirit Spell

It is believed among many Gypsies that if a baby refuses to feed from his mother's breast, a "female spirit of the earth has secretly sucked it." To cure this, according to Leland, an onion is placed between the mother's breasts and the follow-ing incantation is repeated:

"Earth-spirit! Earth-spirit!
Be thou ill.
Let thy milk be fire!
Burn in the earth!
Flow, flow, my milk!
Flow, flow, white milk!
Flow, flow, as I desire
To my hungry child!"

Gypsy Witch-Drum Divination

In Hungary, Gypsies are said to be able to divine the death or recovery of any ill person or animal, as well as discover the location of stolen property, by special use of an instrument known as a "witch-drum." Described by Leland as "a kind of rude tambourine covered with the skin of an animal, and marked with stripes which have a special meaning," a witch-drum is traditionally made from wood that is cut on Whitsunday.

The way in which this instrument is used for divination is as follows: First, nine to 21 thorn apple seeds are arranged on top of the drum and then the tambourine is tapped by a small hammer that is held in the diviner's left hand. (Some diviners simply use their left hand, instead of a hammer, to do the tapping.) After this is done, the position that the seeds take on the markings is then interpreted.

Chapter 9:
Magick in Bloom

"Great minds have puzzled over exactly why Spells and Rituals work as they do, and the only answer which has been reached is that although they undeniably do work with a mysterious efficiency, the reasons for this have yet to be discovered."—Frater Malek, *The Mysterious Grimoire of Mighty Spells and Rituals*

Like the art of magick itself, herbs can be used to heal or to harm. They can inspire dreams or provoke nightmares. They can summon angelic beings or the most demonic of entities. Herbs can also please the palate, soothe the spirit, and fire the imagination.

Herbs can be found in bubbling cauldron brews or burning aromatically upon altars at the witching hour. They are stuffed into poppets, added to the wax of homemade spell candles, brewed into magickal teas, and used as tools for revealing the future and the unknown.

Planting an Astrological Herb Garden

To make an astrological herb garden (based on herbalist Nicholas Culpepper's 17th century astrological classification of plants), divide a planting area into seven sections to represent the Sun, the Moon, and the planets Mars, Mercury, Jupiter, Venus, and Saturn.

In the section dedicated to the Sun, plant any of the following Sun-ruled herbs on a Sunday when the Moon is waxing and the planetary hour corresponds to the Sun: angelica, chamomile, lovage, rosemary, rue, St. John's wort, or saffron.

In the section dedicated to the Moon, plant any of the following Moon-ruled herbs on a Monday when the Moon is waxing and the planetary hour corresponds to the Moon: lettuce, moonwort, purslane, or saxifrage.

In the section dedicated to the planet Mars, plant any of the following Mars-ruled herbs on a Tuesday when the Moon is waxing and the planetary hour corresponds to Mars: basil, garlic, horseradish, or rhubarb.

In the section dedicated to the planet Mercury, plant any of the following Mercury-ruled herbs on a Wednesday when the Moon is waxing and the planetary hour corresponds to Mercury: calamint, caraway, dill, elecampane, fennel, horehound, lavender, or parsley.

In the section dedicated to the planet Jupiter, plant any of the following Jupiter-ruled herbs on a Thursday when the Moon is waxing and the planetary hour corresponds to Jupiter: agrimony, asparagus, avens, borage, chervil, houseleek, sage, or sweet cicely.

In the section dedicated to the planet Venus, plant any of the following Venus-ruled herbs on a Friday when the Moon is waxing and the planetary hour corresponds to Venus: coltsfoot, mints, motherwort, mugwort, pennyroyal, strawberry, vervain, violets, or yarrow.

In the section dedicated to the planet Saturn, plant any of the following Saturn-ruled herbs on a Saturday when the Moon is waxing and the planetary hour corresponds to Saturn: bistort, comfrey, mullein, Solomon's seal, or wintergreen.

A Garden to Weave a Web of Love

To create a garden of love enchantment, plant any combination of the following herbs traditionally associated with love-attraction on a Friday when the moon is new, waxing, or full. (Friday is the day of the week ruled by the goddess Venus, and the appropriate time for any magickal undertakings involving love.)

Herbs of love: Adam and Eve, apple, basil, cardamom, catnip, cherry, coltsfoot, coriander, daffodil, daisy, damiana, devil's bit, gardenia, gentian, geranium, hibiscus, High John the Conqueror, hyacinth, jasmine, juniper, lady's mantle, lavender, lemon verbena, linden, lovage, love seed, maidenhair fern, mandrake, meadowsweet, moonwort, myrtle, oleander, orchid, pansy, peach, peppermint, plumeria, poppy, raspberry, rose, rosemary, rue, skullcap, spearmint, strawberry, thyme, tomato, trillium, tulip, valerian, vanilla, Venus flytrap, vervain, vetivert, violet, willow, witch grass, wormwood, yarrow.

Hoodoo Spell to Draw the Love of Another

On a Friday when the moon is in its waxing phase and the hour of the day or night is ruled by the planet Venus, place a lucky hand root (the root of an orchid plant) in a small jar filled with rose oil. Seal the jar with a lid, and then enchant it by thrice reciting the following magickal incantation:

> *Waxing moon and Venus hour,*
> *Charge this root with mystic power.*
> *Let it work without ado,*
> *And draw to me a love so true.*

Allow the root to soak in the rose oil for seven consecutive days and nights. On the following Friday when the hour of the day or night is again ruled by Venus, take the lucky hand from the jar of oil and wear it, every day and night, close to your heart.

To ensure that the enchanted lucky hand root does not lose its magickal potency, be sure to anoint it with three drops of the rose oil every Friday during a Venus-ruled hour.

The lucky hand (which is also known as a hand of power, helping hand, and salap) is said to be ruled by Venus and sacred to the goddess after whom this planet is named. It is a popular root among practitioners of hoodoo folk magick in and around the city of New Orleans.

Houseleek Love Spell

To win the heart of another, fill a mojo bag with fresh houseleek while filling your mind with romantic thoughts about the person with whom you are in love. Anoint the bag with three drops of rose oil or any love-attracting occult oil, and then wear it every day and every night as close to your heart as possible.

For maximum effectiveness, be sure to begin this spell when the moon is new. Refill the mojo bag with fresh herbs and re-anoint it every three days.

Spell to Gain a New Lover

An old and very simple hoodoo love spell calls for wood aloes to be burned on a night when the moon is full and shining brightly. If your will is strong and you have the utmost faith in your magick, a new lover will come into your life before the next new moon.

Love Enchantment

Beth root (also known as trillium and Indian root) has long been used in the art and practice of love enchantment. Rub one upon your naked body when the moon is waxing and the planetary hour is under the domain of Venus, and this will help you to attract a new lover.

To cast a love enchantment over a particular person, secretly mix a pinch of dried and powdered Beth root into the food or drink of the person whom you desire. (For best results, be sure to do this on a Friday when the moon is waxing.) After consuming it, he or she will soon begin to take an interest in you. However, love magick can only do so much, and it is up to you to win his or her heart.

Spell to Increase Male Potency

According to an old hoodoo spell from New Orleans, an infusion of trumpet weed (also known as joe-pye weed) will help to increase a man's sexual potency when rubbed upon his erect member. The best time to work this spell is when the moon is in a waxing phase. Do not attempt when the moon is waning, otherwise opposite results may be attained.

The Lucky 13 Herb Garden

To create a garden to magickally attract good luck into your life and keep bad luck at bay, plant any 13 herbs from the following list on a Thursday (ruled by the planet Jupiter) when the moon is waxing or full. Do not plant when the moon is waning (growing smaller) otherwise you may cause your good luck to wane.

Good luck herbs: aloe vera, bamboo, be-still, bluebell, cabbage, calamus, China berry, chinchona, daffodil, devil's bit, fern, grains of paradise, hazel, heather, holly, houseleek, huckleberry,

Irish moss, Job's tears, lucky hand, oak, pomegranate, poppy, purslane, rose, snakeroot, star anise, strawberry, sumbul, vetivert, violet, wood rose.

Chinese Wealth Spell

An old Chinese spell to increase one's luck and wealth calls for three coins to be wrapped in red paper and then buried in the soil of a potted plant with round (not pointed) leaves. The larger the plant, the more potent the spell is said to be.

Additionally, the time of the new moon is the best time at which to perform this spell. It is also important that you keep the plant healthy and happy, and take care to remove all fading or dead leaves at once. Should you fail to do this, the positive effects from the spell may be reversed.

Hops for Prosperity and Good Luck

The hop, a plant commonly employed as a flavoring and preservative in beer since the 14th century, has long been regarded by Witches as an herb of prosperity and good luck.

It is an old custom among the English to hang a spray of flowering hops in the kitchen or dining room to ensure the prosperity of all in the household.

Many Witches and other magickal practitioners believe that hops possess healing energy vibrations and use the plant's flowers and leaves to stuff healing poppets and sachets. Dried hops are also added to magickal incenses and burned during the casting of spells to help heal many ailments.

To help cure insomnia and ward off nightmares, stuff a pillowcase with dried hops that have been enchanted by visualization and incantation. Sleep with the herb-stuffed pillow beneath your head and you should enjoy a peaceful night's rest.

To attract good luck, as well as to keep bad luck away, fashion a wreath from dried hops and keep it in your home over the mantelpiece or the hearth. Be sure to replace it with a new wreath every year at hop-picking season to prevent your good luck from running out.

Spells to Win a Court Case

If you are involved in a court case and are in need of a little magickal assistance, perform any of the following hoodoo spells to ensure that the judge will rule in your favor:

Mix a pinch of the herb known as black candle tobacco with a bit of salt, and then burn it along with a black candle prior to going to court.

It is said that courtroom victory is awarded to those who bathe in a tub of water into which a lovage root has been added.

Brewing a tea from cascara sagrada (also known as sacred bark) and then sprinkling it around the courtroom prior to your proceeding will also help you to win your case.

If mojo magick suits you, anoint either a Chewing John root or the root of a snakeroot plant with three drops of Court Room Oil (a powerful hoodoo oil available in many occult shops and Witchcraft supply catalogues. If you are unable to obtain this particular oil, you may use High John the Conqueror Oil in its place.) Place the root inside a mojo bag and then carry or wear it when you go to court.

For another highly effective mojo, burn some dried galangal every night during the two weeks preceding your court case and save the ashes in a green flannel bag. Anoint the bag with three drops of Court Room Oil, and then wear or carry it on you when you go in to face the judge.

The Spirit Garden

To create a spirit garden to attract wandering spirits, take some dirt from a graveyard when the moon is full and mix it into the soil of your garden area. After doing this, plant any of the following herbs associated with the summoning of spirits: dandelion, pipsissewa, sweet grass, thistle, tobacco, wormwood.

To create a garden devoted to a particular spirit, plant all the flowers and plants that the deceased person was fond of in life, and, if at all possible, place something in the garden that once belonged to him or her. If the person was cremated and you are in possession of the ashes, open the urn and sprinkle a bit of the remains over the garden. Mix it into the soil with a gardening implement or your fingers if you desire. If the person was given a burial, try to obtain a small amount of dirt from the grave and then mix it into the soil of the spirit garden.

Plant the garden on the anniversary of the person's birth or death, or some other day of the year bearing a special meaning to that person (such as a wedding anniversary). It is important that you create it with loving energies and not those of sadness and mourning. As you plant the garden and each time you water it, turn all your thoughts to the person to whom the garden is dedicated. When you feel his or her presence growing stronger around you, you will know that you've connected with their spirit. Should their ghost be observed in or near the garden, let not your heart be struck with fear. Offer up loving emotions and comforting words. Ghosts are almost always in need of love and comfort.

Herbs for Conjuring and Banishing

Witches and ceremonial magicians alike have long used the following herbs in a variety of ways to conjure forth both good and evil spirits of the dead.

Herbs for conjuring spirits: Althea, anise, balsam tree, bamboo, catnip, dandelion, elder, gardenia, mint, pipsissewa, sandalwood, sweetgrass, thistle, tobacco, willow, wormwood.

Herbs for banishing spirits: agrimony, angelica, arbutus, asafetida, avens, bean, birch, boneset, buckthorn, clove, clover, cumin, devil's bit, dragons blood, elder, fern, fleabane, frankincense, fumitory, garlic, heliotrope, horehound, horseradish, juniper, leek, lilac, mallow, mint, mistletoe, mullein, myrrh, nettle, onion, peach, peony, pepper, pine, rosemary, rue, sage, sandalwood, sloe, snapdragon, tamarisk, thistle, witch grass, yarrow.

To Summon a Spirit

Using dragon's blood ink, write upon a piece of dried bark from a willow tree the name of the person whose spirit you wish to summon. Using a mortar and pestle, crush the bark and then mix it with an equal amount of dried and crushed sandalwood.

At the witching hour when the moon is on the wane, place a cauldron at a deserted crossroads and burn the bark mixture within it. Call upon the goddess Hecate to assist you in this rite, and then summon the spirit by thrice reciting the following incantation:

Spirit of the dead,
I call you to me
By the power of goddess Hecate.
Hear me, o spirit,
Awaken from thy rest.
In human form now manifest!

To make a spirit rise from its resting place and speak, necromancers and sorcerers from long ago would steal into a graveyard in the dark of a moonless night and burn a dried and powdered wormwood and sandalwood mixture over the grave of a dead person.

Traditionally, the spirit would be made to visibly appear within the confines of a magick circle or triangle ritually drawn upon the ground.

Herbal Spells to Ward Off Evil Spirits

According to occult belief, performing any of the following simple spells with a strong conviction will work to keep all evil spirits and demons at bay:

1. Burn a dried ginseng root.
2. Carry fennel seeds in a mojo bag.
3. Hang fennel over your doors and windows.
4. Wear the root of a devil's shoestring around your neck.
5. Shake a hollowed-out gourd filled with dried beans.
6. Plant holly around your home.
7. Wear or carry an orrisroot or peony root as a protective amulet.
8. Hang some plantain or periwinkle above your front door and windows.
9. Burn a sage smudge wand.
10. Sprinkle an infusion of vervain around the perimeter of your property.

Another old method used by European Witches and Christians alike to ward off evil spirits called for St. John's wort to be gathered on St. John's Day (June 24th). The herb would then be hung above the doors and windows of houses and barns to prevent evil spirits from gaining entry. When worn or carried in a mojo bag, St. John's wort was believed to guard against the most evil of spirits, as well as all demonic entities.

A Charm to Ward Off Dark Spirits of the Night

For protection against evil-natured spirits while you sleep, fill a red mojo bag with cinquefoil (also known as five-finger grass). Hang it above your bed and anoint it every Sunday at sunrise with three drops of any occult oil designed for protection.

Cinquefoil gathered on the morning of the Summer Solstice also works well to keep succubus and incubus demons at bay, and ensures restful sleep throughout the night.

Protection Garden

To create a garden to magickally protect your home and family against evil influences, enemies, and misfortune, plant near your home a garden filled with any of the following plants believed throughout the centuries to possess mystical protective powers. Sunday is the best day of the week to plant this garden. It is ruled by the Sun, which astrologically governs all form of protection.

Herbs possessing protective qualities: acacia, African violet, aloe vera, angelica, anise, arbutus, basil, bay, bittersweet, bloodroot, boneset, cactus, carnation, cinquefoil, clove, clover, datura, devil's bit, devil's shoestring, dill, elecampane, fennel, fern, foxglove, garlic, geranium, hazel, heather, holly, honeysuckle, horehound, houseleek, hyacinth, hyssop, ivy, juniper, kava-kava, lady's slipper, lavender, leek, lilac, lily, linden, loosestrife, lucky hand, mandrake, marigold, masterwort, meadow rue, mint, mugwort, mulberry, mullein, oak, orris, parsley, pennyroyal, peony, pepper tree, periwinkle, pimpernel, pine, primrose, purslane, radish, ragwort, raspberry, rose, rosemary, rowan, sage, St. John's wort, sandalwood, snapdragon, thistle, toadflax, tormentil, tulip, valerian, vervain, violet, willow, witch hazel, wolf's bane, woodruff, wormwood, and yucca.

Hex-Breaking

Among many Witches in Europe and America, the hydrangea is prized as a plant possessing natural hex-breaking powers. To counter or ward off hexes, wear or carry a mojo bag filled with hydrangea bark and anointed with three drops of any occult oil designed for the preventing or removing of hexes.

If you are convinced that a hex has been placed upon your home, you can easily counter it by scattering powdered hydrangea bark around the premises when the moon is in its waning phase. In addition, burn some dried hydrangea bark in a censer and use the smoke to fumigate each room.

Wormwood Curses and Charms

Wormwood is a dual-purpose herb that has long been used by Witches and other magickal folks to send curses as well as to protect against them.

In the southern region of the United States, it is not uncommon for a hoodoo practitioner to seek revenge against an enemy by sprinkling a bit of dried and powdered wormwood upon the individual's path when the moon is waning. According to hoodoo belief, wormwood causes strife and misfortune to befall those who tread upon it or upon whose footprints it is sprinkled.

To protect yourself against curses, hexes, and all kinds of jinxes, wear or carry a mojo bag filled with wormwood and anointed daily with three drops of any occult oil designed for protection against black magick.

Spells for Your Next-Door Enemies

In a perfect world there would be no such thing as noisy, nosy, trespassing, troublesome, rude, or gossiping neighbors. But alas, we live not in such a perfect world and often find ourselves living next door to an individual or family whose mission it seems is to make our lives as miserable as they possibly can. (There is an old saying that "high fences make good neighbors" and I have had my share of neighbors in the past that more than deserved to have this old adage tattooed across their foreheads!) Luckily, when all else fails, there are a number of magickal tricks that a Witch can turn to.

Sprinkling a bit of bittersweet or the herb known as berry-of-the-fish in your neighbor's yard when the moon is waning is said to cause them to pack up their belongings and move away. At the very least, this spell will cause them to leave you in peace.

When the moon is on the wane, throw a handful of adder's tongue or slippery elm into the yard of a neighbor to stop them from slandering or spreading gossip about you.

Note: It is important to remember that what goes around comes around. So perform a revenge spell ONLY if you have just cause to do so, and ONLY after all other options have been exhausted. Never put a "whammy" on anyone just for the fun of it or to prove to them or to yourself that you have the power to do it. Wise Witches know that frivolous magick is for fools.

For protection against a jealous neighbor, wear or carry a mojo bag containing garlic cloves and/or plantain. Both of these herbs have long been used by mojo practitioners as protective charms against those possessed by the "green-eyed monster."

Spell to Banish a Roommate

One thing worse than living next door to an obnoxious person would surely have to be living under the same roof with one!

One tried-and-true method to make someone move out of your home is to make a brew from an herb known as jenjible.

When the moon is waning, sprinkle it upon all items of clothing belonging to the person you wish to be rid of. You can also secretly add the brew to the wash water when your roommate's clothes are being washed. Within a short period of time, he or she will be looking for a new place to live!

A Woman's Spell to Hex a Cruel Man

If a woman desires to place a hex on a man who has treated her in a cruel fashion, she should carry out the following spell on a night when the moon is waning and the sky is dark and void of stars. A night that hosts a raging storm is even better!

Anoint a jezebel root with Jezebel Oil, and then sprinkle Destierro powder upon it while stating and visualizing your intent. Place the root inside a small jar and then seal it with a lid. Wrap the jar in a piece of black cloth, secure it with a black cord, and then secretly bury it in the yard of the man at who your hex is directed.

Should you decide later to lift the hex, unearth the jar while clearly stating your intent (such as, "From Mother Earth I remove this jar so that the hex upon [man's name] shall be no more."). Smash the jar with a rock marked with a white pentagram. Burn the jezebel root and then scatter its ashes to the wind.

An Ancient Spell to Quell a Tempest

The following ash tree spell hails from the Gospelles of Dystaues (first published in the year 1507): "When some tempest doth aryse in the ayer we oughte anone to make a fyre of foure [stakes] of an ashe tree in crosse wyse aboue the wynde and thenne afterwarde make a crosse upon it, and anone the tempest shall [be] torne a syde."

A Garden of Fairy Enchantments

To create a magickal garden for the fairy folk to call home, or to attract them to an existing garden, be sure to plant some flowers that are fairy favorites. These include butterfly bush, carnations (particularly red ones), clover, coreopsis, cosmos, cowslips, daisies, foxglove, hollyhock, hyssop, lavender, lobelia, pansies, petunias, primroses (particularly blue and red ones), roses (all types), shamrock, thyme, vervain, yarrow, and zinnias.

Fairies are said to dance in rings around certain trees when a full moon illuminates the night sky. Some fairies also like to make their homes within or underneath trees. The following trees are fairy favorites, and planting one or more in or near your garden is sure to attract the wee folk: alder, apple, ash, aspen, blackthorn, bramble, broom, elder, hawthorn, holly, juniper, lilac, oak, osier, pine, and silver birch.

If your garden happens to contain dill, morning glory, peonies, prickly gorse, or rosemary, it would be advisable to remove these plants (or transplant them to another location) if you wish to make your garden inviting to fairies. According to herbal lore, fairies are greatly repulsed by the sight 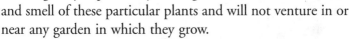 and smell of these particular plants and will not venture in or near any garden in which they grow.

Fairies are fond of the sight and sound of bubbling water, and it is for this reason that they can often be glimpsed frolicking merrily near fountains and brooks. A garden containing a fountain of any size or style, a birdbath, or a fishpond is most appealing to fairies. Straw is also said to be effective in attracting fairies, as are the enchanting melodies conjured by windchimes caressed by a gentle breeze. Fairy statues or garden gnomes situated among the flowers and trees also send out inviting vibrations to the fairies and let them know that their presence is welcome in your garden.

A Witch's Wishing Well Garden

To create a magickal wishing well garden, plant around a well any of the following plants traditionally used by Witches and other magickal practitioners to make secret wishes manifest: bamboo, beech, buckthorn, dandelion, dogwood, grains of paradise, hazel, Job's tears, pomegranate, sage, sandalwood, sunflower, tonka, violet, walnut.

If you have no access to a well, simply place a small wooden rain barrel or earthenware pot in the center of the garden and fill it with water. Either will make a suitable substitute for an actual wishing well.

When the moon is full and her silver rays call to you to make magick, go to the wish garden and toss a coin into the well (or other container of water) as you state your wish and visualize it. Be sure not to tell your wish to anyone, otherwise it may not come true.

Chapter 10:
A Garden of Dreams

Since the dawn of mankind, herbs have played a significant role in the practice of dream magick, most commonly being used for inducing dreams of a prophetic nature and giving protection to those who sleep and dream. Herbs have been utilized as charms to prevent nightmares and ward off demons that prey upon sleeping mortals, stuffed into dream pillows and brewed into magickal teas and potions to bring restful sleep, and made into magickal incense and burned prior to bedtime.

Herbs Associated with Dream Magick

The following list contains many of the herbs traditionally used by Witches and other magickal folks in dream magick, followed by their various applications:

Anise

To prevent nightmares, fill a white mojo bag with as many anise seeds as it can possibly hold, and then sew it to the inside of your pillowcase. This simple, yet effective, Witch's spell from the Middle Ages is said to ensure pleasant dreams. Scatter the leaves of an anise plant around your bedroom to keep yourself protected against evil influences while you sleep.

Ash

To induce dreams of a prophetic nature, place seven leaves from an ash tree beneath your pillow before going to sleep. The ash tree, which was sacred to the ancient Teutons and symbolic of their mythological "world tree" known as Ygdrasill, is also said to offer protection against nightmares, dreamcurses, and all psychic attacks that occur while one is asleep and most vulnerable.

Bay

To induce dreams of a prophetic nature, place bay leaves beneath your pillow before going to sleep. It is said that bay leaves, when cast into a fire on a night of the full moon, can enable one to see the future in a dream. The use of bay in divinatory rites and dream magick can be traced back to the ancient Greeks, who believed it to be sacred to their god Apollo.

Bracken

If you are faced with a problem to which you cannot find a solution, an old magickal spell suggests placing the root of a bracken underneath your pillow just before you go to sleep. Occult folklore holds that the root of this plant will bring forth a dream that will contain the answer you seek. In addition, many Witches and other magickal practitioners use bracken for protection against evil and negative influences.

Buchu

To induce dreams of a prophetic nature, mix a pinch of dried buchu leaves with a pinch of frankincense. On a night of the full moon, light a charcoal block (which can be bought at most occult shops and religious supply stores), place it in a fireproof incense burner, and then sprinkle a small amount of the herbal mixture upon it. For best results, do this in your bedroom prior to bedtime.

Cedar

When burned as incense, the wood of the cedar is said to "cure the predilection to having bad dreams," according to the late author Scott Cunningham in his book, *Cunningham's Encyclopedia of Magical Herbs*. Sleep with cedar twigs beneath your pillow to help awaken or strengthen your psychic powers. A cedar branch hung above your bed will protect you against evil forces while you sleep.

Cinquefoil

Also known by the folk-name "five-finger grass," the cinquefoil is said to assure restful sleep when put into a blue mojo bag and suspended from the bedpost. Place a sprig of cinquefoil containing seven leaflets beneath your pillow before going to sleep in order to dream about the man or woman who is destined to be your marriage mate. This simple method of amatory dream divination is centuries old.

Heliotrope

To induce dreams of a prophetic nature, place some heliotrope leaves beneath your pillow prior to bedtime. A full moon is the ideal lunar phase in which to do this. If you have had personal possessions stolen from you and desire to know whom the thief is, heliotrope may help to induce a dream that reveals the true identity of the culprit.

Holly

An old Witch's method to induce prophetic dreams is as follows: Without speaking a single word, gather together nine holly leaves at the witching hour (midnight) on a Friday. Wrap them in a white cloth and then tie nine knots in it. Place the charm beneath your pillow prior to bedtime, and whatever dreams you experience during the night are likely to come true.

Huckleberry

According to Scott Cunningham's *Encyclopedia of Magical Herbs*, "To make all your dreams come true, burn the leaves [of a huckleberry plant] in your bedroom directly before going to sleep." After seven days have passed, that which you have dreamt shall be made manifest.

Hyacinth

For the prevention of nightmares, grow a hyacinth plant in a pot and keep it as close to your bed as possible. When dried and burned as incense prior to bedtime, the fragrant flowers of the hyacinth are said to help induce pleasant dreams. Should you awaken from a depressing dream or nightmare, the smell of a hyacinth in bloom will help to lift your spirits.

Jasmine

For restful sleep and pleasant dreams, sleep with a blue mojo bag filled with jasmine flowers beneath your pillow or sewn to the inside of your pillowcase. Scott Cunningham says, "the flowers are smelled to induce sleep." To induce dreams of a prophetic nature, burn a bit of dried jasmine in an incense burner in your bedroom just before you go to sleep.

Lemon Verbena

For a dreamless slumber, fill a gray-colored charm bag with lemon verbena and wear it on a string around your neck when you go to sleep. Additionally, drinking a bit of the juice extracted from the plant is said to help suppress dreams.

Mandrake

The mandrake is unquestionably the most magickal of all plants, and the part of it most commonly employed in the casting of spells is its mysterious root, which bears a curious resemblance to the human form. It is said that sleep can be induced by the mere scent of a mandrake root, and when one is suspended from the headboard of a bed, the sleeper is guarded against all manner of harm—both natural and supernatural. Rub a mandrake root upon your Third Eye chakra before sleeping to induce a prophetic dream of your future lover or marriage mate. *Caution*: Mandrake possesses strong narcotic properties. Handle with care and do not ingest any part of the plant!

Marigold

To induce dreams of a prophetic nature, scatter the flowers of a marigold under and around your bed before turning in for the evening. This plant is also said to induce dreams that reveal the true identities of thieves, as well as to offer protection against sorcerers who work their black magick through dreams.

Mimosa

To induce dreams of a prophetic nature, fill a blue or yellow mojo bag with mimosa flowers and then place it beneath your pillow before you go to sleep. According to author Rosemary Ellen Guiley in *The Encyclopedia of Witches and Witchcraft*, blue is the color associated with psychic and spiritual awareness, and prophetic dreams. However, in his book on magickal herbs, Scott Cunningham lists yellow as the color corresponding to divination, psychic powers, and visions. I, personally, have always used blue or purple for this purpose, but you may use whichever color feels right for you. In addition, anointing your Third Eye chakra with an infusion of mimosa prior to sleeping helps to facilitate dreams containing prophecies.

Mistletoe

When placed beneath a pillow at bedtime or put into a white mojo bag and attached to the bedpost or headboard, the leaves and berries of the mistletoe plant are said to prevent nightmares and insomnia from interfering with one's sleep. In keeping with ancient Druidic tradition, use mistletoe that has been harvested with a golden blade on either Midsummer or the sixth day following the new moon.

Morning Glory

To safeguard your sleep against nightmares, according to occult tradition, fill a white mojo bag with the seeds of a morning glory plant and place it beneath your pillow just before going to bed. In addition, morning glory seeds can be added, either alone or with other dream-magick herbs (such as anise, mistletoe, mullein, purslane, rosemary, or vervain), to dream pillows for the same purpose.

Mugwort

Of all the herbs associated with dream magick, mugwort is by far the most popular and the most potent. To induce dreams of a prophetic nature, stuff a dream pillow with mugwort leaves and then rest your head upon it to sleep. Other ways in which to induce dreams that reveal the unknown or things that are yet to be include the drinking of mugwort tea and the anointing of the Third Eye chakra with a dab of mugwort juice. Mugwort can also be made into an incense, which, when burned prior to sleeping, aids in astral projection and lucid dreaming, and summons forth dreams that facilitate spiritual and psychic growth.

Mullein

To prevent nightmares, stuff a white mojo bag with mullein leaves and then place it beneath your pillow just before bedtime.

According to herbal folklore from centuries gone by, mullein also protects a sleeping person from all manner of evil and negativity. Hang mullein over your bedroom door and windows to keep nocturnal incubus and succubus demons at bay.

Onion

To induce dreams of a prophetic nature, place a white onion underneath your pillow before bedtime. This practice is believed to have originated in ancient Egypt, where the onion was at one time regarded as being highly sacred. For protection against evil influences while you sleep, cut an onion in half and keep it close to your bed. Many modern-day practitioners of herbal folk magick continue to subscribe to the old belief that halved or quartered onions work to absorb evil, negativity, and disease.

Peony

For protection against incubus demons, fill a white mojo bag with peony roots, coral, and flint, and then anoint it with three drops of myrrh oil. Pin the mojo bag to your nightgown or pajamas, or attach it to a string around your neck, and wear it throughout the night as you sleep. Rest assured that no incubus would be able to seduce you.

Peppermint

To induce dreams of a prophetic nature, many Witches stuff dream pillows with the fragrant leaves of the peppermint plant. According to an herbal from olden times, the scent of peppermint "compels one toward sleep," which is beneficial should you happen to suffer from insomnia or other sleep disorders.

Purslane

To keep recurring nightmares from interfering with your sleep, place a handful of purslane flowers and leaves beneath your pillow prior to bedtime. According to occult tradition from centuries gone by, this herb also works to ward off evil spirits that prey upon sleeping mortals.

Rose

It is said that success in all matters of the heart awaits those who see a red rose in their dreams. If a single woman picks a red rose on a Midsummer's Eve and sleeps with it tucked between her bosom, the man destined to be her future husband will appear to her in a dream.

Rosemary

To prevent nightmares, sleep with a mojo bag filled with rosemary beneath your pillow. It is said that he (or she) who sleeps with rosemary underneath the bed will be protected from all manner of harm while sleeping. To prevent a dead person's restless spirit from haunting you by way of your dreams, cast a sprig of rosemary into his or her grave. According to occult lore, this will enable the spirit to rest peacefully.

St. John's Wort

One of the most beloved magickal herbs of the ancients, the St. John's wort has enabled many a young lady to capture a glimpse of her future marriage mate in a dream. To accomplish this, place this herb beneath your pillow before going to sleep. It does not matter which part of the plant you use, for all parts of the St. John's wort are potent in magickal workings.

Tobacco

Many Native Americans believe that nightmares are capable of causing physical ailments and disease. To keep this from happening to you, go directly to a stream immediately upon waking from a bad dream and cleanse your body in the running water. Afterwards, in keeping with tradition, cast a handful of tobacco leaves into the stream as an offering to the spirit of the water.

Vervain

To prevent nightmares, place a handful of vervain leaves in your bed, wear them in a mojo bag on a string around your neck, or brew them into a tea and drink it just before bedtime. To induce dreams of a prophetic nature, anoint your Third Eye chakra with vervain juice on a night of the full moon. Close your eyes, open your mind, and allow yourself to drift off to sleep. Upon waking from your slumber, take care to write your dream down on paper (or use a tape recorder) to prevent it from later being forgotten. If interpreted correctly, it will provide you with an insight to events of the future.

Wood Betony

To prevent nightmares or unpleasant visions from interfering with your sleep, pick some leaves from a wood betony plant and then place them beneath your pillow just before going to bed. When scattered on the floor under and around your bed, wood betony leaves are said to keep all evil and negative influences at bay.

Yarrow

Witches and diviners alike have long used the yarrow plant in a number of different ways to induce prophetic dreams pertaining to future marriage mates. The divinatory power of this herb is legendary throughout much of the world, and its strong magickal vibrations have made it a staple of folk magick since ancient times.

Dream Interpretation

Formally known as "oneiromancy," the interpretation of dreams and nightmares to predict events of the future is one of the oldest and simplest forms of divination known to mankind.

Long before Carl Jung and Sigmund Freud began their studies and analyses of the dream-state, it was widely believed that existing within every dream was a doorway leading to a supernatural dimension in which clues to reveal the mysteries of the past, the present, and the future could be found.

Not all dreams are prophetic in nature. However, there are some dreams that do come true, especially those that are repeated three nights in a row, according to occult folklore. Some speak to us in a very direct fashion, while others conceal their messages behind a language of arcane symbolism that requires deciphering before an understanding can be gained.

Dreams have been defined as "visions during sleep," and each one is said to hold its own particular significance. Where dream symbols are concerned, they abound in the thousands, if not hundreds of thousands. Their meanings, according to dream interpretation author Gustavus Hindman Miller, are "as varied, as intricate, and as infinite as our thoughts."

However, this chapter will focus solely on the various dream symbols that relate to herbs and other plants, including flowers and trees. Many of the interpretations herein have been gathered from a number of sources (namely Gustavus Hindman Miller's *10,000 Dreams Interpreted*, Nerys Dee's *The Dreamer's Workbook*, and Ann Ree Colton's *Watch Your Dreams*), and some are my own personal interpretations.

Dream Dictionaries

One final, and perhaps the most important, thing that you should be made aware of before proceeding any further is the fact that accurate dream readings cannot always be formulated by relying solely on the interpretations found within so-called dream dictionaries. Some of these books are based on the occult or metaphysical nature of dreams, while others are based on their psychological nature. However, neither should be viewed as being written in stone, for different dream symbols will often represent different things to different persons.

This is not to say that dream dictionaries have no value or cannot be beneficial for helping one to unlock the mysteries of his or her dreams. Quite the contrary. But if you should ever find yourself feeling that the symbols in your dreams are speaking to you in a different way than suggested by a book of dream interpretations, you should probably disregard the book and pay close attention to what your inner self may be trying to tell you. I offer this advice to those in all areas of interpretation, for when it comes to the mantic arts, nothing can take the place of one's own intuitive powers.

Adam and Eve Roots

To dream about Adam and Eve roots (which are popular amulets among many magickal practitioners skilled in the art of love magick) is said to be a message to the dreamer to carefully consider his or her romantic feelings towards a certain person of the opposite gender.

Apple Blossoms

To dream about apple blossoms is said to be an indication of "spiritual fruits" to come. However, to dream about the actual fruits of an apple tree is believed by some dream interpreters to serve as a warning not to give into temptation.

Arbutus

To dream about an arbutus is said to be an indication of a new beginning for the dreamer. In some cases it may signify the healing power of Mother Nature, or purification.

Belladonna

To dream about belladonna (deadly nightshade) "portends that strategic moves will bring success in commercial circles," according to Gustavus Hindman Miller. For a woman hoping to win the affections of a particular gentleman, this dream supposedly warns that her best efforts will be in vain. As the belladonna is a poisonous plant with a name that translates to "fair lady," it seems more logical to me that a dream in which this plant appears is a warning to the dreamer to beware of a woman whose evil intentions are veiled behind a facade of beauty and charm.

Bleeding Heart

To dream about a bleeding heart is believed by some dream interpreters to be a foretelling of sorrow and suffering for the dreamer, and especially pertaining to affairs of the heart.

Bouquet

To dream about a bouquet of beautiful, fragrant flowers indicates that the dreamer will soon be rewarded for his or her past work and effort. In some instances, it indicates that there will be a joyous family reunion or other happy gathering taking place in the near future.

To dream about a bouquet of black or wilted flowers is said to be an extremely bad omen presaging a grave illness or the death of a loved one.

Briers, Brambles, and Thorns

To dream about being caught in a tangled mass of prickly plants and unable to free yourself is said to be an extremely unlucky sign. Such a dream often warns of enemies and/or evil forces at work. However, if you dream that you are successful in freeing yourself from the entangling briers or brambles, this indicates that you will stand victorious in overcoming your enemies and averting any and all evil forces that may be threatening you.

Thorns almost always portend something bad on the horizon when they make an appearance in our dreams. Thorns camouflaged by green foliage or beautiful flowers may be a warning to the dreamer to beware of secret enemies.

Carnation

To dream about a carnation is said to symbolize a "rebirth" of some kind for the dreamer. If you are in need of hope or are trying to make a fresh start in life, a dream involving a carnation may prove to be a very lucky sign for you.

Chrysanthemum

To dream about chrysanthemums of any color but black or white is indicative of pleasant engagements. Seeing or gathering white chrysanthemums is generally believed to foretell loss and sorrow. To dream about black ones, as it is to dream about most black flowers, is said by many dream interpreters to portend the death of a loved one.

Clover

To dream about clover is said to foretell happiness for the dreamer, and also signify the end of losing streaks for those who gamble. A dream involving finding or picking a four-leaf clover indicates phenomenal good luck in the offing, and in some cases, a wish that will soon be fulfilled.

Cowslips

To dream about cowslips in full bloom is said to portend a divorce or the ending of a love affair. To dream that you are gathering cowslips is said to indicate an unpleasant estrangement between seemingly close friends. In his book, *10,000 Dreams Interpreted*, Gustavus Hindman Miller refers to dreams in which cowslips are seen growing as "sinister."

Daffodils

To dream about seeing or picking daffodils is said to symbolize happiness and adoration. In the country of Wales it is believed that daffodils appearing in dreams signify fresh hopes for the future.

Dahlia

To dream about brightly colored dahlias is said to indicate good fortune. To dream about a black dahlia (a rare flower said to bloom only once every million years) is a mystical symbol of rebirth, according to some. Others believe it symbolizes Witchcraft or the occult world.

Daisy

To dream about a field of daisies in bloom is said to symbolize love, kindness, hope, and honor. However, dreaming of a bunch of daisies is said to be an omen of sorrow, while dreaming of them out of season supposedly warns of the presence of evil in some guise.

Forest

To dream that you are lost in a forest is said to indicate unhappiness and discord where home and family are concerned. A forest full of dead or broken trees is generally regarded as an unlucky dream omen and said to portend a serious illness or death in one's family. A dream in which you find yourself in an enchanted forest clearly implies that you are living in a fantasy world, refusing to face reality, and so forth.

To dream about a forest on fire is a warning that family quarrels will soon be flaring up. However, if you dream that you are the one who started the blaze, this may indicate that you subconsciously feel responsible for inciting a domestic dispute or family feud.

For poets and writers, a dream that takes place in a forest of majestic trees in foliage is said to be an exceptionally good omen, foretelling fame and public acclaim. See **Trees**.

Forget-Me-Not

To dream about a forget-me-not is said to be a reminder to the dreamer of someone who has been forgotten or neglected. It may also be an important message from beyond the grave. Pay close attention to all symbols appearing in such a dream.

Foxglove

To dream about the foxglove is said to be an indication of a heart condition. Interestingly, the foxglove is a plant from which the heart medication, Digitalis, is derived.

Frangipani

To dream about a frangipani is said to be an omen of a wedding taking place in the near future. Depending upon what other symbols are contained within the dream, the omen may apply to either the dreamer or to someone close to the dreamer.

Garden

To dream about planting a garden is said to be a sign that you will soon be undertaking a new project or venture. For a woman desiring to have a child, a dream involving the planting of seeds in a garden may symbolize conception. Seeing, or walking through a garden of flowers in bloom indicates happiness and peace of mind, unless the flowers are all white, in which case the coming of sorrow is indicated. To dream about seeing, speaking to, or chasing a stranger or trespasser in your garden indicates that someone has been, or will soon be, intruding upon your private life.

For a man to dream about a vegetable garden is said to be an unlucky sign, usually indicating the loss of one's fortune. However, for a woman to dream about seeing, planting, or harvesting vegetables in a garden is said to indicate fame or a marriage blessed by happiness.

Grass

To dream about seeing a field of green grass or a well-manicured lawn indicates happiness as well as a prosperous future in store for the dreamer. However, to dream about grass that is withered, patchy, or blemished by noxious weeds, is said to warn of illness or hard times ahead.

Heliotrope

To dream about a heliotrope is said to indicate the presence of an earthbound entity or a connection of some sort between the dreamer and the world of the dead. Ann Ree Colton states that such a dream may also be "a symbol of an unseen tempter." Pay close attention to all symbols appearing in such a dream.

Hemlock

To dream about hemlock is said to be a warning to the dreamer of dangerous situations and enemies. Take heed, otherwise you may find yourself a victim at the hands of ignorant and brutal men.

Hemp

To dream about hemp is said to be a most favorable sign, indicating success in all endeavors. For individuals in the business world, it promises that financial opportunities are on the horizon. To dream about sowing hemp seed is said to herald the forging of a deep and lasting friendship.

Herbs

To dream about any type of poisonous herb is said to indicate the presence of an enemy. To dream about gathering or using medicinal herbs may serve as a reminder to the dreamer to take better care of his or her health.

High John the Conqueror

To dream about a High John the Conqueror is a sign to the dreamer that he or she will soon achieve a long-awaited and/or hard-earned victory, gain (or regain) control over something or someone, or overcome a difficult situation. The symbol of a High John the Conqueror root in a dream may also serve as a reminder to us that we are the masters of our own destinies.

Honeysuckle

To dream about seeing or gathering honeysuckles is said to be an indication of contentment and prosperity for the dreamer. For a betrothed or newlywed woman, such a dream is believed by many to portend a future blessed with matrimonial bliss.

Ivy

To dream about an ivy-covered house is said to be an indication of good health and financial gains. For a young woman to dream about seeing ivy in the silvery light of the moon indicates that she may soon find herself involved in a secret love affair. Some dream interpreters believe that sorrow or a broken engagement is foretold by dreams in which withered ivy is seen.

Jasmine

To dream about fragrant jasmine flowers is said to portend exquisite, but fleeting, pleasures for the dreamer. The jasmine also denotes feminine qualities, and in some instances may reveal a natural talent for healing.

Lady-Slipper

To dream about a lady-slipper is said to indicate a communion between the dreamer and the mystical realm of fairies.

Laurel

To dream about the laurel is said to be a favorable omen for those desiring fame and success. For a woman to dream that she is placing a wreath of laurel upon the head of her lover indicates that her romantic interest will be true to her. If an athlete should happen to dream about laurel, this is a clear sign that he or she will be victorious in upcoming competition.

Leaves

To dream about leaves on trees is said to be a good omen, especially in the area of one's business affairs. Should your dream happen to involve leaves of gold, this is a sign that success and wealth await you in the near future. To dream about leaves on the ground is said to be an omen of hard times ahead.

Lily

To dream about a lily is believed by some to foretell sorrow, or, in some cases, the coming of bittersweet joys. Some dream interpreters are of the opinion that lilies (including water lilies) portend the death of a loved one when seen in a dream.

Mandrake

To dream about a mandrake plant or root is said to be an indication that occult forces (either of a positive or negative nature) are at work.

The connection between the mandrake and female fertility is one that dates back long before biblical times. Therefore, a dream that involves a mandrake is said to be a very favorable sign for a woman desiring to be with child.

Mistletoe

To dream about mistletoe is said to indicate healing, protection, or good luck in the offing. For a young lady, such a dream may reveal that she will soon be the recipient of a kiss from someone who has taken a fancy to her.

Dream dictionaries vary on their interpretations of the mistletoe dream symbol. Some say it is a favorable omen, indicating great joy and celebration (unless seen with "unpromising signs.") Others say that it represents "a poisonous thought." Ann Ree Colton claims that this plant symbolizes "initiation into the darker Celtic rites" and warns the dreamer "against pagan orgies and their dangers."

Mustard

To dream about a mustard plant is said to foretell happiness and success for those who farm the land, and wealth to those who sail the seas. To dream about a burning sensation being felt in your mouth after eating mustard seed warns against making a hasty decision that you will later live to regret. It is said that if a young lady dreams about eating mustard, she will find herself giving up wealth in exchange for personal desires.

Narcissus

To dream about a narcissus is said to be an indication of a narcissistic, conceited, or self-absorbed nature. The narcissus derives its name from a young man of Greek legend who drowned after falling in love with his own reflection in a pool of water. Upon his death, he was transformed into a flower by the gods who dwelled atop Mount Olympus.

Nutmeg

To dream about nutmeg is said to be an indication of a prosperous future for the dreamer. It is a very good sign to dream about nutmeg prior to embarking on a journey, for some diviners of dreams believe that the symbol of the nutmeg foretells safe and pleasant travels.

Opium Poppy

To dream about an opium poppy (or the narcotic from which it is extracted) is said to be a warning to be wary of sly and seductive strangers who will bring misfortune upon you. Also beware of being tricked into submission. See **Poppy**.

Parsley

To dream about parsley is said to be an indication of a hard-earned success. To dream that you are eating parsley is a favorable sign, usually indicating good health.

Pepper

To dream about black pepper in a peppershaker is said to be an omen of quarrels soon to take place. The grinding of black pepper in a mill warns that the dreamer will fall victim to the trickeries of others if he or she is not careful. If a young lady dreams that she is adding black pepper to her food, this often indicates the presence of false friends. To dream about seeing or growing a red pepper plant is said to indicate a marriage partner who possesses an independent nature and is thrifty when it comes to the spending of money. Be warned that you will end up "burned" by your own gossiping tongue should you happen to dream about burning your tongue or mouth while eating black or red pepper.

Peppermint

To dream about peppermint is said to be an indication of pleasurable experiences and interesting affairs. Some dream interpreters believe that a dream in which peppermint appears foretells a romantic interlude soon to take place for the dreamer.

Poppy

According to Ann Ree Colton, a dream or meditation in which a poppy appears warns against "an insidious or habit-forming influence demoting the will." See **Opium Poppy**.

Roots

To dream about seeing the roots of plants or trees is said to be an indication of stability, confidence, and strength of purpose. Uprooted plants or trees presage a change of residence in the future for the dreamer. Some dream interpreters believe that illness or sorrow is foretold by dreams that involve the medicinal use of roots.

Rose

To dream about a red rose is said to be a sign of true love. If a woman dreams that she is picking a red rose, this is an indication that she will receive a marriage proposal sometime in the very near future.

To dream about seeing a black rose is said to be a sign that the powers of black magick are at work around you. Dreams involving white roses, as well as dead rosebushes, are believed by many dream interpreters to foretell grave illnesses and, in some cases, the death of a loved one.

To dream of being pricked by a rose thorn is an omen of an emotional or physical suffering soon to occur. And there is a good chance that you may soon find yourself the victim of another's deceit should you dream that your lover places a rose in your hair.

Rosemary

To dream about rosemary is believed by some diviners of dreams to indicate the coming of sorrow and indifference, especially for families whom appear blessed by prosperity.

Saffron

To dream about saffron is said to be a warning against bitter enemies who are secretly plotting against you. Also, do not entertain false hopes. To dream that you are drinking a cup of saffron tea is usually indicative of family quarrels brewing.

Sage

To dream about sage, either as a living plant or as a culinary herb, is said to indicate that a healing is taking place for the dreamer on a physical level. Being an herb strongly linked to protection in both the realms of magick and myth, sage may also be a sign to the dreamer that he or she is under protection, or is in need of protection, depending upon the circumstances of the dream and how the sage relates to them.

Snapdragon

To dream about snapdragons is said to be a sign that the dreamer should expect the unexpected. In some instances, such a dream may serve as a warning not to let one's self be overcome by impulsiveness.

Thistle

To dream about a thistle is said to be an omen of hard times ahead for the dreamer.

Trees

To dream about cedar, oak, or pine trees is said to be an indication of great prosperity and success in an undertaking. Palms and bay laurel trees indicate happiness and leisure. To dream about a poplar tree that is leafy or in bloom is a sign of good luck.

Wealth and happiness are foretold by dreams involving juniper trees, but only after the dreamer has experienced sorrow, according to some dream interpreters. For individuals suffering from an illness or injury, the juniper is a good omen, indicating a speedy recovery. For those who have found disappointment in love, it promises a bright future.

It is said that dreaming about a yew tree is a grim omen. Be prepared for a disappointment of some sort, or possibly a bout of ill health. Some diviners of dreams believe that dreaming about a dead yew heralds a death in the family.

A dream involving the branches of a tree is said to symbolize the branches or members of the dreamer's "family tree." See **Forest**.

Weeds

To dream about a garden or lawn that is overgrown with weeds is said to be an omen of difficult times ahead. In some instances, it may also be trying to express to the dreamer that he or she has been neglecting something important.

To dream that you are pulling weeds indicates that you must work harder on overcoming certain obstacles before being able to proceed with your plans. To dream that others are pulling weeds is said to be a warning that adversaries will attempt to thwart your plans.

Weeping Willow

To dream about a weeping willow tree is said to portend sorrow or a sad journey in the near future.

Wreath

To dream about a wreath of fresh flowers is a very lucky sign for the dreamer. A bridal wreath indicates that an uncertain engagement will soon result in a happy ending. A wreath of wilted flowers is a warning of ill health or "wounded love," and one consisting entirely of black flowers or black leaves is said to portend the news of a death.

Zinnia

To dream about a zinnia is said to be an omen of spinsterhood for an unmarried woman.

Chapter 11:
Herbal Correspondences

The Magick of Herbs

Lavender and fragrant rose,
The fertile seeds of love it sows.
Mugwort for a Samhain scrying;
Hemlock for a broomstick flying.
Rowan tree to ward off harm;
High John for a mojo charm;
Hazel for a wand conductive;
Lovage root for spells seductive.
Yarrow's good for divination;
Devil's-bit for good vibrations;
Rue and dill to evil quell;
And mandrake for a wondrous spell.
—from *Priestess and Pentacle*
by Gerina Dunwich

In this section you will find close to 250 different plants arranged alphabetically by their common names. Each listing herein contains the plant's botanical name (in Latin), its Pagan folk name/s (if known), type (perennial, annual, or biennial), planetary and elemental rulers, and the Pagan gods and goddesses that the plant is associated with in myth or magick.

Acacia
Botanical name: *Acacia Senegal*
Plant type: deciduous evergreen shrub
Planetary ruler: Sun
Elemental ruler: Air
Sacred to: Astarte, Diana, Ishtar, Osiris, and Ra

Adam and Eve roots
Botanical name: *Orchis* spp.
Plant type: perennial
Planetary ruler: Venus
Elemental ruler: Water
Sacred to: Venus, Aphrodite

Acacia

Adder's Tongue
Botanical name: *Erythronium americanum*
Plant type: perennial
Planetary ruler: Moon in Cancer
Elemental ruler: Water

African Violet
Botanical name: *Saintpaulia ionantha*
Plant type: perennial
Planetary ruler: Venus
Elemental ruler: Water

Agaric
Botanical name: *Amanita muscaria*
Pagan name: death angel
Plant type: mushroom
Planetary ruler: Mercury
Elemental ruler: Air
Sacred to: Dionysus

Adder's Tongue

Agrimony

Botanical name: *Agrimonia eupatoria*
Plant type: perennial
Planetary ruler: Jupiter in Cancer
Elemental ruler: Air

Ague Root

Botanical name: *Aletris farinosa*
Pagan names: devil's-bit and unicorn root
Plant type: perennial

Agrimony

Alfalfa

Botanical name: *Medicago sativa*
Plant type: perennial
Planetary ruler: Venus
Elemental ruler: Earth

Allspice

Botanical name: *Pimenta officinalis*
Plant type: tropical evergreen
Planetary ruler: Mars
Elemental ruler: Fire

Almond

Botanical name: *Prunus dulcis*
Plant type: deciduous tree
Planetary ruler: Mercury
Elemental ruler: Air
Sacred to: Attis, Hermes, Mercury, and Thoth

Almond

Aloe Vera

Botanical name: *Aloe vera*
Plant type: perennial
Planetary ruler: Moon
Elemental ruler: Water

Anemone
Botanical name: *Anemone patens*
Plant type: perennial
Planetary ruler: Mars
Elemental ruler: Fire
Sacred to: Adonis, Venus

Angelica
Botanical name: *Angelica archangelica*
Plant type: perennial (or 3-year "biennial")
Planetary ruler: Sun in Leo
Elemental ruler: Fire
Sacred to: Venus

Angelica

Anise
Botanical name: *Pimpinella anisum*
Plant type: annual
Planetary ruler: Jupiter
Elemental ruler: Air

Apple
Botanical name: *Pyrus*
Pagan names: Fruit of the Gods, Fruit of the Underworld
Plant type: deciduous tree
Planetary ruler: Venus
Elemental ruler: Water
Sacred to: Aphrodite, Apollo, Athena, Diana, Dionysus,
          Hera, Iduna, Olwen, Venus, and Zeus

Apricot
Botanical name: *Prunus armeniaca*
Plant type: deciduous tree
Planetary ruler: Venus
Elemental ruler: Water
Sacred to: Venus

Apricot

Asafetida

Botanical name: *Ferula assafoetida*
Pagan name: devil's dung
Plant type: perennial
Planetary ruler: Mars
Elemental ruler: Fire

Ash

Ash

Botanical name: *Fraxinus excelsior*
Plant type: deciduous tree
Planetary ruler: Sun
Elemental ruler: Fire
Sacred to: Gwydion, Mars, Neptune, Poseidon, Thor,
       Uranus, and Woden

Aspen

Botanical name: *Populus* spp.
Plant type: deciduous tree
Planetary ruler: Mercury
Elemental ruler: Air

Aster

Botanical name: *Callistephus chinesis*
Pagan name: starwort
Plant type: perennial
Planetary ruler: Venus
Elemental ruler: Water
Sacred to: Venus

Aster

Avens

Botanical name: *Geum urbanum*
Pagan name: star of the earth
Plant type: perennial
Planetary ruler: Jupiter
Elemental ruler: Fire

Avocado
Botanical name: *Persea americana*
Plant type: evergreen tree or shrub
Planetary ruler: Venus
Elemental ruler: Water

Bachelor's Buttons
Botanical name: *Centaurea cyanus*
Pagan name: devil's flower
Plant type: annual or biennial
Planetary ruler: Venus
Elemental ruler: Water

Bachelor's Buttons

Balm of Gilead
Botanical name: *Commiphora opobalsamum*
Plant type: deciduous tree
Planetary ruler: Venus
Elemental ruler: Water

Bamboo
Botanical name: *Bambusa vulgaris*
Plant type: perennial
Sacred to: Hina

Banyan
Botanical name: *Ficus benghalensis*
Pagan name: Indian god tree
Plant type: deciduous tree
Planetary ruler: Jupiter
Elemental ruler: Air
Sacred to: Maui

Barley

Barley
Botanical name: *Hordeum* spp.
Plant type: annual

Planetary ruler: Venus
Elemental ruler: Earth

Basil

Basil

Botanical name: *Ocimum basilicum*
Pagan name: witches herb
Plant type: annual
Planetary ruler: Mars
Elemental ruler: Fire
Sacred to: Erzulie, Vishnu

Bay Laurel

Botanical name: *Laurus nobilis*
Pagan name: Daphne
Plant type: evergreen tree or shrub
Planetary ruler: Sun
Elemental ruler: Fire
Sacred to: Aesculapius, Apollo, Ceres, Eros, and Faunus

Beans

Belladonna

Botanical name: *Phaseolus vulgaris*
Plant type: annual
Planetary ruler: Mercury
Elemental ruler: Air
Sacred to: Demeter, Cardea

Belladonna (Deadly Nightshade)

Botanical name: *Atropa belladonna*
Pagan names: devil's cherries, sorcerer's berry, and
      witch's berry
Plant type: perennial
Planetary ruler: Saturn
Elemental ruler: Water
Sacred to: Bellona, Circe, and Hecate

Benzoin

Botanical name: *Styrax benzoin*
Plant type: deciduous tree
Planetary ruler: Sun
Elemental ruler: Air

Benzoin

Bergamot (Bee Balm)

Botanical name: *Monarda didyma*
Plant type: perennial
Planetary ruler: Mercury
Elemental ruler: Air

Birch

Botanical name: *Betula alba*
Pagan name: lady of the woods
Plant type: deciduous tree
Planetary ruler: Venus
Elemental ruler: Water
Sacred to: Thor

Bistort

Botanical name: *Polygonum bistorta*
Pagan name: dragonwort
Plant type: perennial
Planetary ruler: Saturn
Elemental ruler: Earth

Bittersweet

Botanical name: *Celastrus scandens*
Plant type: perennial
Planetary ruler: Mercury
Elemental ruler: Air

Bittersweet

Black Hellebore

Botanical name: *Helleborus niger*
Plant type: perennial

Planetary ruler: Saturn
Elemental ruler: Water

Black Pepper
Botanical name: *Piper nigrum*
Plant type: perennial vine
Planetary ruler: Mars
Elemental ruler: Fire

Black Pepper

Black Snakeroot
Botanical name: *Sanicula marilandica*
Plant type: perennial
Planetary ruler: Mars
Elemental ruler: Fire

Blackberry
Botanical name: *Rubus villosus*
Plant type: biennial
Planetary ruler: Venus
Elemental ruler: Water
Sacred to: Brigit

Bladderwrack (Kelp)
Botanical name: *Fucus visiculosus*
Pagan name: sea spirit
Plant type: perennial seaweed
Planetary ruler: Moon
Elemental ruler: Water

Bladderwrack (kelp)

Bleeding Heart
Botanical name: *Dicentra spectabilis*
Plant type: perennial
Planetary ruler: Venus
Elemental ruler: Water

Blessed Thistle
Botanical name: *Carduus benedicta*
Plant type: annual
Planetary ruler: Mars
Elemental ruler: Fire

Bloodroot
Botanical name: *Sanguinaria canadensis*
Plant type: perennial
Planetary ruler: Mars
Elemental ruler: Fire

Bloodroot

Blue Flag
Botanical name: *Iris versicolor*
Plant type: perennial
Planetary ruler: Venus
Elemental ruler: Water

Bodhi
Botanical name: *Ficus religiosa*
Pagan name: sacred tree
Plant type: deciduous tree
Planetary ruler: Jupiter
Elemental ruler: Air
Sacred to: Buddha, Vishnu

Boneset
Botanical name: *Eupatorium perfoliatum*
Plant type: perennial
Planetary ruler: Saturn
Elemental ruler: Water

Boneset

Borage
Botanical name: *Borago officinalis*
Plant type: annual

Planetary ruler: Jupiter
Elemental ruler: Air

Broom
Botanical name: *Cyticus scoparius*
Pagan name: besom
Plant type: deciduous shrub
Planetary ruler: Mars
Elemental ruler: Air

Buckthorn

Buckthorn
Botanical name: *Rhamnus*
Plant type: deciduous tree or shrub
Planetary ruler: Saturn
Elemental ruler: Water

Burdock
Botanical name: *Arctium lappa*
Plant type: biennial
Planetary ruler: Venus
Elemental ruler: Water

Calamus
Botanical name: *Acorus calamus*
Plant type: perennial
Planetary ruler: Moon
Elemental ruler: Water

Caraway
Botanical name: *Carum carvi*
Plant type: biennial
Planetary ruler: Mercury
Elemental ruler: Air

Caraway

Cardamom
Botanical name: *Elettaria cardamomum*
Plant type: perennial
Planetary ruler: Venus
Elemental ruler: Water
Sacred to: Erzulie

Catnip
Botanical name: *Nepeta cataria*
Plant type: perennial
Planetary ruler: Venus
Elemental ruler: Water
Sacred to: Bast

Catnip

Cedar
Botanical name: *Cedrus libani*
Plant type: evergreen tree
Planetary ruler: Sun
Elemental ruler: Fire

Celandine
Botanical name: *Chelidonium majus*
Pagan name: devil's milk
Plant type: biennial or perennial
Planetary ruler: Sun
Elemental ruler: Fire

Centaury
Botanical name: *Centaurium erythraea*
Plant type: annual
Planetary ruler: Sun
Elemental ruler: Fire
Sacred to: Chiron

Celandine

Chamomile
Botanical name: *Chamamelum nobile*
Plant type: perennial
Planetary ruler: Sun
Elemental ruler: Water
Sacred to: Woden

Chamomile

Cherry
Botanical name: *Prunus avium*
Plant type: deciduous tree
Planetary ruler: Venus
Elemental ruler: Water
Sacred to: Venus

Chickweed
Botanical name: *Stellaria media*
Pagan name: starwort
Plant type: annual
Planetary ruler: Moon
Elemental ruler: Water

Chicory
Botanical name: *Cichorium intybus*
Plant type: biennial
Planetary ruler: Sun
Elemental ruler: Air

Chrysanthemum
Botanical name: *Chrysanthemum* spp.
Plant type: annual
Planetary ruler: Sun
Elemental ruler: Fire

Chrysanthemum

Cinnamon

Botanical name: *Cinnamomum zeylanicum*
Plant type: evergreen tree
Planetary ruler: Sun
Elemental ruler: Fire
Sacred to: Aphrodite, Venus

Cinnamon

Cinquefoil (Five Finger Grass)

Botanical name: *Potentilla canadensis*
Plant type: perennial
Planetary ruler: Jupiter
Elemental ruler: Fire

Cleavers (Bedstraw)

Botanical name: *Galium aparine*
Plant type: annual
Planetary ruler: Saturn

Clover

Botanical name: *Trifolium*
Plant type: perennial
Planetary ruler: Mercury
Elemental ruler: Air
Sacred to: Rowen

Clover

Cloves (Clove Tree)

Botanical name: *Syzygium aromaticum*
Plant type: evergreen tree
Planetary ruler: Jupiter
Elemental ruler: Fire

Colewort

Botanical name: *Brassica oleracea*
Plant type: annual or perennial
Planetary ruler: Moon
Elemental ruler: Water

Coltsfoot

Botanical name: *Tussilago farfara*
Plant type: perennial
Planetary ruler: Venus
Elemental ruler: Water

Columbine

Botanical name: *Aquilegia canadensis*
Plant type: perennial
Planetary ruler: Venus
Elemental ruler: Water

Coltsfoot

Comfrey

Botanical name: *Symphytum officiale*
Plant type: perennial
Planetary ruler: Saturn
Elemental ruler: Water

Coriander

Botanical name: *Coriandrum sativum*
Plant type: annual
Planetary ruler: Mars
Elemental ruler: Fire

Corn

Botanical name: *Zea mays*
Pagan name: sacred mother
Plant type: annual
Planetary ruler: Venus
Elemental ruler: Earth

Corn

Sacred to: Centeotl, Ceres, Chicomecohuatl, Cinteotl, Kornjunfer, Krumine, Mother Corn, Onatha, Osiris, Robigo, Robigus, Selu, Xilonen, Xochipilli

Cowslip

Botanical name: *Primula veris*
Pagan name: fairy cup
Plant type: perennial
Planetary ruler: Venus
Elemental ruler: Water
Sacred to: Freya

Cowslip

Crocus

Botanical name: *Crocus vernus*
Plant type: perennial
Planetary ruler: Venus
Elemental ruler: Water

Cubeb

Botanical name: *Piper cubeba*
Plant type: perennial vine
Planetary ruler: Mars
Elemental ruler: Fire

Cucumber

Botanical name: *Cucumis sativus*
Plant type: annual
Planetary ruler: Moon
Elemental ruler: Water

Cumin

Botanical name: *Cumimum cyminum*
Plant type: annual
Planetary ruler: Mars
Elemental ruler: Fire

Cypress

Cypress

Botanical name: *Cupressus sempervirens*
Pagan name: tree of death

Plant type: evergreen tree
Planetary ruler: Saturn
Elemental ruler: Earth
Sacred to: Aphrodite. Apollo, Artemis, Ashtoreth,
        Cupid, Hebe, Hekat, Jupiter, Mithras, Pluto,
        and Zoroaster

Daffodil
Botanical name: *Narcissus* spp.
Plant type: perennial
Planetary ruler: Venus
Elemental ruler: Water

Daffodil

Daisy
Botanical name: *Chrysanthemum leucanthemum*
Plant type: perennial
Planetary ruler: Venus
Elemental ruler: Water
Sacred to: Artemis, Freya, and Thor

Dandelion
Botanical name: *Taraxacum officinale*
Plant type: perennial
Planetary ruler: Jupiter
Elemental ruler: Air
Sacred to: Hecate

Devil's Bit
Botanical name: *Scabiosa succisa*
Plant type: perennial
Planetary ruler: Venus

Dill
Botanical name: *Anethum graveolens*
Plant type: annual

Dandelion

Planetary ruler: Mercury
Elemental ruler: Fire

Dittany of Crete

Botanical name: *Dictamus origanoides*
Plant type: perennial
Planetary ruler: Venus
Elemental ruler: Water

Dock

Dock

Botanical name: *Rumex* spp.
Plant type: perennial
Planetary ruler: Jupiter
Elemental ruler: Air

Dodder

Botanical name: *Cuscuta glomurata*
Pagan name: devil's guts, hellweed, and witches' hair
Plant type: parasitic vine
Planetary ruler: Saturn
Elemental ruler: Water

Dragon's Blood

Botanical name: *Daemonorops draco*
Plant type: palm tree
Planetary ruler: Mars
Elemental ruler: Fire

Elderberry

Elderberry

Botanical name: *Sambucus canadensis*
Pagan names: devil's eye, tree of doom
Plant type: deciduous tree
Planetary ruler: Venus
Elemental ruler: Water
Sacred to: Holda and Venus

Elecampane

Botanical name: *Inula helenium*
Pagan names: elf dock, elfwort
Plant type: perennial
Planetary ruler: Mercury
Elemental ruler: Air

Elm

Botanical name: *Ulmus campestris*
Pagan name: Elven
Plant type: deciduous tree
Planetary ruler: Saturn
Elemental ruler: Water
Sacred to: Hoenin, Lode, and Odin

Elecampane

Endive

Botanical name: *Cichorium endivia*
Plant type: biennial
Planetary ruler: Jupiter
Elemental ruler: Air

Eryngo

Botanical name: *Eryngium* spp.
Plant type: perennial
Planetary ruler: Venus
Elemental ruler: Water

Eyebright

Botanical name: *Euphrasia officinalis*
Plant type: annual
Planetary ruler: Sun
Elemental ruler: Air

Eyebright

Fennel

Botanical name: *Foeniculum vulgare*
Plant type: perennial
Planetary ruler: Mercury
Elemental ruler: Fire
Sacred to: Dionysus and Prometheus

Fennel

Fenugreek

Botanical name: *Trigonella foenum-graecum*
Plant type: annual
Planetary ruler: Mercury
Elemental ruler: Air
Sacred to: Apollo

Feverfew

Botanical name: *Chrysanthemum parthenium*
Plant type: perennial
Planetary ruler: Venus
Elemental ruler: Water

Figwort

Botanical name: *Scrophularia nodosa*
Plant type: perennial
Planetary ruler: Venus
Elemental ruler: Water

Figwort

Flax (Linseed)

Botanical name: *Linum usitatissimum*
Plant type: annual
Planetary ruler: Mercury
Elemental ruler: Fire
Sacred to: Holda

Fleabane

Botanical name: *Inula dysenterica*

Plant type: perennial
Planetary ruler: Venus
Elemental ruler: Water

Foxglove

Botanical name: *Digitalis purpurea*
Pagan names: fairy fingers, fairy petticoats, fairy
thimbles, fairy weed, folk's gloves, witches'
bells, witches' thimbles, and witches' gloves
(*Digitalis lanata*)
Plant type: biennial or perennial
Planetary ruler: Venus
Elemental ruler: Water

Fumitory

Botanical name: *Fumaria officinalis*
Pagan name: earth smoke
Plant type: annual
Planetary ruler: Saturn
Elemental ruler: Earth

Foxglove

Galangal

Botanical name: *Alpinia galanga*
Pagan name: Low John the Conqueror
Plant type: perennial
Planetary ruler: Mars
Elemental ruler: Fire

Garlic

Botanical name: *Allium sativum*
Plant type: perennial
Planetary ruler: Mars
Elemental ruler: Fire
Sacred to: Hecate

Fumitory

Gentian
Botanical name: *Gentiana lutea*
Plant type: perennial
Planetary ruler: Mars
Elemental ruler: Fire

Geranium
Botanical name: *Pelargonium* spp.
Plant type: perennial
Planetary ruler: Venus
Elemental ruler: Water

Ginger

Ginger
Botanical name: *Zingiber officinale*
Plant type: perennial
Planetary ruler: Mars
Elemental ruler: Fire

Ginseng
Botanical name: *Panax ginseng*
Plant type: perennial
Planetary ruler: Sun
Elemental ruler: Fire

Goat's Rue
Botanical name: *Galega officinalis*
Plant type: perennial
Planetary ruler: Mercury
Elemental ruler: Air
Sacred to: Pan

Ginseng

Goldenrod
Botanical name: *Solidago odora*
Plant type: perennial
Planetary ruler: Venus
Elemental ruler: Air

Goldenseal

Botanical name: *Hydrastis canadensis*
Plant type: perennial
Planetary ruler: Sun
Elemental ruler: Fire

Gorse

Botanical name: *Ulex europaeus*
Pagan name: Frey
Plant type: perennial
Planetary ruler: Mars
Elemental ruler: Fire
Sacred to: Jupiter, Thor

Hawthorn

Hawthorn

Botanical name: *Crataegus oxacantha*
Pagan name: hagthorn
Plant type: deciduous tree or shrub
Planetary ruler: Mars
Elemental ruler: Fire
Sacred to: Cardea, Flora, and Hymen

Hazel

Botanical name: *Corylus* spp.
Plant type: deciduous tree or shrub
Planetary ruler: Sun
Elemental ruler: Air
Sacred to: Artemis, Diana, Mercury, and Thor

Heather

Botanical name: *Calluna vulgaris*
Plant type: perennial
Planetary ruler: Venus
Elemental ruler: Water
Sacred to: Isis

Heather

Heliotrope
Botanical name: *Heliotropium peruvianum*
Plant type: annual
Planetary ruler: Sun
Elemental ruler: Fire
Sacred to: Apollo

Hemlock
Botanical name: *Conium maculatum*
Pagan name: warlock weed
Plant type: biennial
Planetary ruler: Saturn
Elemental ruler: Water
Sacred to: Hecate

Hemlock

Hemp
Botanical name: *Cannabis sativa*
Plant type: annual
Planetary ruler: Saturn
Elemental ruler: Water

Henbane
Botanical name: *Hyosycamus niger*
Pagan name: devil's-eye and Jupiter's bean
Plant type: annual or biennial
Planetary ruler: Saturn
Elemental ruler: Water

Hibiscus
Botanical name: *Hibiscus* spp.
Plant type: annual
Planetary ruler: Venus
Elemental ruler: Water

Henbane

High John the Conqueror

Botanical name: *Ipomoea jalapa*
Plant type: annual vine
Planetary ruler: Mars
Elemental ruler: Fire

Holly

Botanical name: *Ilex aquifolium*
Pagan name: bat's wings
Plant type: evergreen shrub
Planetary ruler: Mars
Elemental ruler: Fire

Honeysuckle

Honeysuckle

Botanical name: *Lonicera caprifolium*
Plant type: perennial
Planetary ruler: Jupiter
Elemental ruler: Earth

Hops

Botanical name: *Humulus lupulus*
Plant type: perennial
Planetary ruler: Mars
Elemental ruler: Air

Horehound

Botanical name: *Marrubium vulgare*
Pagan name: seed of Horus
Plant type: perennial
Planetary ruler: Mercury
Elemental ruler: Air
Sacred to: Horus

Hops

Horse Chestnut

Botanical name: *Aesculus* spp.

Plant type: deciduous tree

Planetary ruler: Jupiter

Elemental ruler: Fire

Horseradish

Botanical name: *Armoracia rusticana*

Plant type: perennial

Planetary ruler: Mars

Elemental ruler: Fire

Honeysuckle

Hound's-Tongue

Botanical name: *Cynoglossum officianle*

Pagan name: gypsy flower

Plant type: biennial

Planetary ruler: Mars

Elemental ruler: Fire

Houseleek

Botanical name: *Sempervivum tectorum*

Plant type: perennial

Planetary ruler: Jupiter

Elemental ruler: Air

Hyacinth

Botanical name: *Hyacinthus orientalis*

Plant type: perennial

Planetary ruler: Venus

Elemental ruler: Water

Hyssop

Botanical name: *Hyssopus officinalis*

Plant type: perennial

Planetary ruler: Jupiter

Elemental ruler: Fire

Houseleek

Iris

Botanical name: *Iris* spp.
Plant type: perennial
Planetary ruler: Venus
Elemental ruler: Water
Sacred to: Iris and Juno

Jasmine

Ivy

Botanical name: *Hedera helix*
Plant type: evergreen vine
Planetary ruler: Saturn
Elemental ruler: Water
Sacred to: Bacchus, Dionysus, and Osiris

Jasmine

Botanical name: *Jasminum officinale*
Pagan name: moonlight on the grove
Plant type: evergreen vine
Planetary ruler: Moon
Elemental ruler: Water
Sacred to: Vishnu

Jimsonweed

Botanical name: *Datura* spp.
Pagan names: devil's apple, ghost flower, sorcerer's
       herb, witches' thimble, and *yerba del diablo*
       (Spanish: herb of the devil)
Plant type: annual
Planetary ruler: Saturn
Elemental ruler: Water

Juniper

Botanical name: *Juniperus communis*
Plant type: evergreen tree or shrub

Jimsonweed

Planetary ruler: Sun
Elemental ruler: Fire

Kava-Kava
Botanical name: *Piper methysticum*
Plant type: perennial
Planetary ruler: Saturn
Elemental ruler: Water
Sacred to: Lono, Kanaloa, and Kane

Kava-kava

Knotweed
Botanical name: *Polygonum aviculare*
Plant type: annual
Planetary ruler: Saturn
Elemental ruler: Earth

Lady's Mantle
Botanical name: *Alchemilla vulgaris*
Plant type: perennial
Planetary ruler: Venus
Elemental ruler: Water

Lady's Slipper
Botanical name: *Cypripedium pubescens*
Plant type: perennial
Planetary ruler: Saturn
Elemental ruler: Water

Larkspur
Botanical name: *Delphinium* spp.
Plant type: annual
Planetary ruler: Venus
Elemental ruler: Water

Larkspur

Lavender

Botanical name: *Lavendula officinale*
Pagan name: elf leaf
Plant type: perennial
Planetary ruler: Mercury
Elemental ruler: Air

Lavender

Leek

Botanical name: *Allium* spp.
Plant type: perennial
Planetary ruler: Mars
Elemental ruler: Fire

Lemon Grass

Botanical name: *Cymbopogon citratus*
Plant type: perennial
Planetary ruler: Mercury
Elemental ruler: Air

Lemon Verbena

Botanical name: *Lippia citrodora*
Plant type: perennial
Planetary ruler: Mercury
Elemental ruler: Air

Licorice

Botanical name: *Glycyrrhiza glabra*
Plant type: perennial
Planetary ruler: Venus
Elemental ruler: Water

Lily

Botanical name: *Lilium* spp.
Plant type: perennial
Planetary ruler: Moon

Lily

Elemental ruler: Water
Sacred to: Juno, Kwan Yin, Nepthys, and Venus

Lily of the Valley

Botanical name: *Convallaria magalis*
Plant type: perennial
Planetary ruler: Mercury
Elemental ruler: Air
Sacred to: Aesculapius and Apollo

Lobelia

Botanical name: *Lobelia inflata*
Plant type: annual or biennial
Planetary ruler: Saturn
Elemental ruler: Water

Lobelia

Loosestrife

Botanical name: *Lythrum salicaria*
Plant type: perennial
Planetary ruler: Moon
Elemental ruler: Earth

Lotus

Botanical name: *Nelumbo nucifera*
Plant type: perennial
Planetary ruler: Moon
Elemental ruler: Water

Lovage

Botanical name: *Levisticum officinale*
Pagan name: love root
Plant type: perennial
Planetary ruler: Sun
Elemental ruler: Fire

Lotus

Lucky Hand

Botanical name: *Orchis* spp.
Pagan name: hand of power
Plant type: perennial
Planetary ruler: Venus
Elemental ruler: Water

Lucky Hand

Maidenhair Fern

Botanical name: *Adiantum pedatim*
Plant type: perennial
Planetary ruler: Venus
Elemental ruler: Water
Sacred to: Venus

Mandrake

Botanical name: *Mandragora officinale*
Pagan names: herb of Circe, *hexenmannchen* (German:
    witches' mannikin), mandragora, and
    zauberwurzel (German: sorcerer's root)
Plant type: perennial
Planetary ruler: Mercury
Elemental ruler: Fire
Sacred to: Hathor and Hecate

Marigold

Botanical name: *Calendula officinalis*
Plant type: annual
Planetary ruler: Sun
Elemental ruler: Fire

Marjoram

Marjoram

Botanical name: *Origanum majorana*
Plant type: perennial
Planetary ruler: Mercury

Elemental ruler: Air
Sacred to: Aphrodite and Venus

Masterwort
Botanical name: *Imperatoria ostruthium*
Plant type: perennial
Planetary ruler: Mars
Elemental ruler: Fire

May Apple
Botanical name: *Podophyllum peltaltum*
Pagan name: American mandrake
Plant type: perennial
Planetary ruler: Mercury
Elemental ruler: Fire

May Apple

Meadowsweet
Botanical name: *Spiraea filipendula*
Plant type: perennial
Planetary ruler: Jupiter
Elemental ruler: Air

Milk Thistle
Botanical name: *Carduus marianus*
Plant type: annual or biennial
Planetary ruler: Mars
Elemental ruler: Fire

Mints
Botanical name: *Mentha* spp.
Plant type: perennial
Planetary ruler: Mercury
Elemental ruler: Air
Sacred to: Hecate and Pluto

Mints

Mistletoe
Botanical name: *Viscum album*
Pagan name: devil's fuge, Druid's herb, golden bough, and witches' broom
Plant type: evergreen parasitic plant
Planetary ruler: Sun
Elemental ruler: Air
Sacred to: Apollo, Freya, Frigga, Odin, and Venus

Morning Glory
Botanical name: *Ipomoea hederacea*
Pagan name: bindweed
Plant type: annual vine
Planetary ruler: Saturn
Elemental ruler: Water

Mugwort
Botanical name: *Artemisia vulgaris*

Mistletoe

Pagan name: cronewort
Plant type: perennial
Planetary ruler: Venus
Elemental ruler: Earth
Sacred to: Artemis and Diana

Mullein
Botanical name: *Verbascum thapsus*
Pagan names: graveyard dust, hag's tapers, and Jupiter's staff
Plant type: biennial
Planetary ruler: Saturn
Elemental ruler: Fire
Sacred to: Jupiter

Mullein

Mustard

Botanical name: *Brassica* spp.
Plant type: annual
Planetary ruler: Mars
Elemental ruler: Fire
Sacred to: Aesculapius

Nutmeg

Botanical name: *Myristica fragrans*
Plant type: evergreen tree
Planetary ruler: Jupiter
Elemental ruler: Fire

Nutmeg

Oak

Botanical name: *Quercus alba*
Pagan name: Jove's nuts
Plant type: deciduous tree
Planetary ruler: Sun
Elemental ruler: Fire
Sacred to: Cybele, Dagda, Diana, Erato, Hecate, Herne
       Janus, Jupiter, Pan, Rhea, Thor, and Zeus

Oats

Botanical name: *Avena sativa*
Plant type: annual
Planetary ruler: Venus
Elemental ruler: Earth

Oleander

Botanical name: *Nerium oleander*
Plant type: perennial
Planetary ruler: Saturn
Elemental ruler: Earth

Oleander

Olive

Botanical name: *Olea europaea*
Plant type: evergreen tree
Planetary ruler: Sun
Elemental ruler: Fire
Sacred to: Apollo, Athena, Irene, Minerva,
and Ra

Olive

Onion

Botanical name: *Allium cepa*
Plant type: perennial or biennial
Planetary ruler: Mars
Elemental ruler: Fire
Sacred to: Isis

Opium Poppy

Botanical name: *Papaver somniferum*
Plant type: annual
Planetary ruler: Mon
Elemental ruler: Water
Sacred to: Demeter and Hypnos

Orchid

Botanical name: *Orchis* spp.
Pagan name: satyrion
Plant type: perennial
Planetary ruler: Venus
Elemental ruler: Water

Orris Root

Botanical name: *Iris florentina*
Plant type: perennial
Planetary ruler: Venus
Elemental ruler: Water
Sacred to: Aphrodite, Hera, Iris, Isis, and Osiris

Opium Poppy

Pansy

Botanical name: *Viola tricolor*
Plant type: annual
Planetary ruler: Saturn
Elemental ruler: Water

Pansy

Papyrus

Botanical name: *Cyperus papyrus*
Plant type: perennial
Planetary ruler: Mercury
Elemental ruler: Air

Parsley

Botanical name: *Petroselinum sativum*
Pagan name: devil's oatmeal
Plant type: biennial
Planetary ruler: Mercury
Elemental ruler: Air
Sacred to: Persephone

Passionflower

Botanical name: *Passiflora incarnata*
Plant type: herbaceous vine
Planetary ruler: Venus
Elemental ruler: Water

Patchouli

Botanical name: *Pogostemon cablin*
Plant type: perennial
Planetary ruler: Saturn
Elemental ruler: Earth

Pennyroyal

Pennyroyal

Botanical name: *Mentha pulegium*
Plant type: perennial

Planetary ruler: Mars

Elemental ruler: Fire

Peony

Botanical name: *Paeonia officinalis*

Plant type: perennial

Planetary ruler: Sun

Elemental ruler: Fire

Peony

Peppermint

Botanical name: *Mentha piperita*

Plant type: perennial

Planetary ruler: Mercury

Elemental ruler: Fire

Sacred to: Pluto

Periwinkle

Botanical name: *Vinca minor*

Pagan names: devil's eye and sorcerer's violet

Plant type: perennial

Planetary ruler: Venus

Elemental ruler: Water

Pine

Botanical name: *Pinus* spp.

Plant type: evergreen tree

Planetary ruler: Mars

Elemental ruler: Air

Sacred to: Astarte, Attis, Cybele, Dionysus, Pan,
     Sylvanus, and Venus

Periwinkle

Plantain

Botanical name: *Plantago major*

Plant type: perennial

Planetary ruler: Venus

Elemental ruler: Earth

Poke
Botanical name: *Phytolacca americana*
Plant type: perennial
Planetary ruler: Mars
Elemental ruler: Fire

Pomegranate
Botanical name: *Punica granatum*
Plant type: deciduous tree
Planetary ruler: Mercury
Elemental ruler: Fire
Sacred to: Ceres and Persephone

Pomegranate

Potato
Botanical name: *Solanum tuberosum*
Plant type: annual
Planetary ruler: Moon
Elemental ruler: Earth

Primrose
Botanical name: *Primula vulgaris*
Plant type: perennial
Planetary ruler: Venus
Elemental ruler: Earth
Sacred to: Freya

Purslane
Botanical name: *Portulaca oleracea*
Plant type: annual
Planetary ruler: Moon
Elemental ruler: Water

Quince
Botanical name: *Cydonia oblonga*
Plant type: deciduous tree

Purslane

Planetary ruler: Saturn

Elemental ruler: Earth

Ragwort

Botanical name: *Senecio* spp.

Pagan name: fairies' horses

Plant type: perennial

Planetary ruler: Venus

Elemental ruler: Water

Ragwort

Raspberry

Botanical name: *Rubus idaeus*

Plant type: biennial

Planetary ruler: Venus

Elemental ruler: Water

Rhubarb

Botanical name: *Rheum officinale*

Plant type: perennial

Planetary ruler: Venus

Elemental ruler: Earth

Rose

Botanical name: *Rosa* spp.

Plant type: perennial

Planetary ruler: Venus

Elemental ruler: Water

Sacred to: Adonis, Aurora, Cupid, Demeter, Eros,
        Harpocrates, Hathor, Holda, and Isis

Rosemary

Rosemary

Botanical name: *Rosemarinus officinalis*

Pagan name: elf leaf

Plant type: perennial

Planetary ruler: Sun

Elemental ruler: Fire

Rowan (Mountain Ash)

Botanical name: *Sorbus aucuparia*

Pagan name: Thor's helper, witchbane, witchen, and
        witchwood

Plant type: deciduous tree

Planetary ruler: Sun

Elemental ruler: Fire

Sacred to: Thor

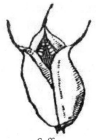

Saffron

Rue

Botanical name: *Ruta graveolens*

Plant type: perennial

Planetary ruler: Mars

Elemental ruler: Fire

Sacred to: Aradia and Diana

Saffron

Botanical name: *Crocus sativa*

Plant type: perennial

Planetary ruler: Sun

Elemental ruler: Fire

Sacred to: Ashtoreth and Eos

Sage

Botanical name: *Salvia officinalis*

Plant type: perennial

Planetary ruler: Jupiter

Elemental ruler: Air

Sage

St. John's Wort

Botanical name: *Hypericum perforatum*

Pagan name: scare-devil

Plant type: perennial

Planetary ruler: Sun

Elemental ruler: Fire
Sacred to: Baldur

Sandalwood

Botanical name: *Santalum album*
Plant type: evergreen tree
Planetary ruler: Moon
Elemental ruler: Water

Sarsaparilla

Botanical name: *Smilax aspera*
Plant type: perennial
Planetary ruler: Jupiter
Elemental ruler: Fire

Sandalwood

Sassafras

Botanical name: *Sassafras albidum*
Plant type: deciduous tree
Planetary ruler: Jupiter
Elemental ruler: Fire

Sesame

Botanical name: *Sesamum indicum*
Plant type: annual
Planetary ruler: Sun
Elemental ruler: Fire
Sacred to: Ganesha

Skullcap

Botanical name: *Scutellaria galericulata*
Plant type: perennial
Planetary ruler: Saturn
Elemental ruler: Water

Sassafras

Snakeroot
Botanical name: *Aristolochia serpentaria*
Plant type: perennial
Planetary ruler: Mars
Elemental ruler: Fire

Solomon's Seal
Botanical name: *Polygonatum officinale*
Plant type: perennial
Planetary ruler: Saturn
Elemental ruler: Water

Snakeroot

Southernwood
Botanical name: *Artemisia abrotanum*
Plant type: perennial
Planetary ruler: Mercury
Elemental ruler: Air

Spikenard
Botanical name: *Inula conyza*
Plant type: perennial
Planetary ruler: Venus
Elemental ruler: Water

Star Anise
Botanical name: *Illicum verum*
Plant type: evergreen tree
Planetary ruler: Jupiter
Elemental ruler: Air

Strawberry
Botanical name: *Fragaria vesca*
Plant type: perennial
Planetary ruler: Venus
Elemental ruler: Water
Sacred to: Freya

Strawberry

Sugar Cane

Botanical name: *Saccharum officinarum*
Plant type: perennial
Planetary ruler: Venus
Elemental ruler: Water

Sunflower

Botanical name: *Helianthus annuus*
Plant type: annual
Planetary ruler: Sun
Elemental ruler: Fire
Sacred to: Sol

Sunflower

Tamarind

Botanical name: *Tamarindus indica*
Plant type: evergreen tree
Planetary ruler: Saturn
Elemental ruler: Water

Tansy

Botanical name: *Tanacetum vulgare*
Plant type: perennial
Planetary ruler: Venus
Elemental ruler: Water

Tea

Botanical name: *Camellia* spp.
Plant type: evergreen tree or shrub
Planetary ruler: Sun
Elemental ruler: Fire

Tansy

Thyme

Botanical name: *Thymus vulgaris*
Plant type: perennial
Planetary ruler: Venus
Elemental ruler: Water

Tobacco
Botanical name: *Nicotiana tobacum*
Plant type: annual or biennial
Planetary ruler: Mars
Elemental ruler: Fire
Sacred to: Earthmaker, the Great Spirit, Kee-shay-lum-
      moo-kawng , Kitche Manitou, Tabuldak, Otoe,
      Tobacco Maiden, Tobacco Spirit, and Wenebojo

Tormentil
Botanical name: *Potentilla tormentilla*
Plant type: perennial
Planetary ruler: Sun
Elemental ruler: Fire
Sacred to: Thor

Tormentil

Trailing Arbutus
Botanical name: *Arbutus unede*
Plant type: evergreen shrub
Planetary ruler: Mars
Elemental ruler: Fire
Sacred to: Cardea

Trillium
Botanical name: *Trillium* spp.
Plant type: perennial
Planetary ruler: Venus
Elemental ruler: Water

Tulip
Botanical name: *Tulipa* spp.
Plant type: perennial
Planetary ruler: Venus
Elemental ruler: Earth

Tulip

Valerian

Botanical name: *Valeriana officinalis*
Pagan name: All-Heal
Plant type: perennial
Planetary ruler: Venus
Elemental ruler: Water

Vervain

Botanical name: *Verbena officinalis*
Pagan name: enchanter's plant, herb of enchantment,
        Juno's tears, and van-van
Plant type: perennial
Planetary ruler: Venus
Elemental ruler: Earth
Sacred to: Aradia, Cerridwen, Isis, Juno, Jupiter, Mars,
        Thor, and Venus

Vervain

Vetivert (Khus-Khus)

Botanical name: *Vetiveria zizanioides*
Plant type: perennial
Planetary ruler: Venus
Elemental ruler: Earth

Violet

Botanical name: *Viola odorata*
Plant type: perennial
Planetary ruler: Venus
Elemental ruler: Water

Willow

Willow

Botanical name: *Salix alba*
Pagan names: tree of enchantment and witches' aspirin
Plant type: deciduous tree
Planetary ruler: Moon

Elemental ruler: Water

Sacred to: Artemis, Belili, Belinus, Ceres, Hecate, Hera, Mercury, and Persephone

Wintergreen

Botanical name: *Gaultheria procumbens*

Plant type: perennial

Planetary ruler: Moon

Elemental ruler: Water

Wintergreen

Witch Grass

Botanical name: *Agropyron repens*

Pagan name: witches' grass

Plant type: perennial grass

Planetary ruler: Jupiter

Witch Hazel

Botanical name: *Hamamelis virginica*

Plant type: deciduous shrub

Planetary ruler: Sun

Elemental ruler: Fire

Wolf's Bane (Monkshood)

Botanical name: *Aconitum napellus*

Pagan name: Cupid's car and Thor's hat

Plant type: perennial

Planetary ruler: Saturn

Elemental ruler: Water

Sacred to: Hecate

Witch Hazel

Wood Betony

Botanical name: *Stachys officinalis*

Plant type: perennial

Planetary ruler: Jupiter

Elemental ruler: Fire

Wood Sorrel

Botanical name: *Oxalis acetosella*
Pagan name: fairy bells
Plant type: perennial
Planetary ruler: Venus
Elemental ruler: Earth

Woodruff

Botanical name: *Galium odorata*
Plant type: perennial
Planetary ruler: Mars
Elemental ruler: Fire

Wormwood

Botanical name: *Artemisia absinthium*
Plant type: perennial
Planetary ruler: Mars
Elemental ruler: Fire
Sacred to: Artemis, Diana, and Iris

Woodruff

Yarrow

Botanical name: *Achillea millefolium*
Pagan names: death flower, devil's nettle, and eerie
Plant type: perennial
Planetary ruler: Venus
Elemental ruler: Water

Chapter 12:
Where to Buy
Magickal Herbs

Alchemy Works Seeds and Herbs

P.O. Box 3455
Sarasota, Florida 34230
(941) 359-9447
www.alchemy-works.com

AzureGreen

P.O. Box 48
Middlefield, Massachusetts 01243
(413) 623-2155
Fax: (413) 623-2156
www.Azuregreen.com

Black Kat Herbals

P.O. Box 271
Smithville, Tennessee 37166
(615) 597-1270
Fax: (615) 597-9430

Botanica Esoterica

712 Broadway
Brooklyn, New York 11206
(800) 567-5555

Coven Gardens

P.O. Box 1064
Boulder, Colorado 80306
(303) 444-4322

Desert Alchemy

P.O. Box 44189
Tucson, AZ 85733
Fax: (520) 325-8405
www.desert.alchemy.com

Devonshire Apothecary

2105 Ashby
Austin, Texas 78704
(512) 444-5039

Enchanted Herbs

6600 Gretna Avenue
Whittier, California 90601
(562) 699-1555

Esoterica

541 Rue Dumaine
New Orleans, Louisiana 70116
(504) 581-7711
(800) 353-7001
www.onewitch.com

Eye of the Cat

3314 E. Broadway
Long Beach, Ca. 90803
(562) 438-3569
Fax: (562) 439-1176
www.eyeofthecat.com/index.htm

Firewind Herbal Products

P.O. Box 5527
Hopkins, Minnesota 55343
(877) 950-3330
(952) 543-9065
www.firewindhp.com

Full Moon Botanicals

409 E. Church Street
Sandwich, Illinois 60548
(815) 786-6222
http://alternativemarketplace.com/showcase/fullmoon.htm

Gaia Garden Herbal Dispensary

2672 West Broadway
Vancouver, British Columbia V6K 2G3
Canada
(604) 734-4372
Fax: (604) 734-4376

Gnostic Garden

P.O. Box 242
Newcastle upon Tyne, NE99 1ED
England
www.gnosticgarden.com

Green Dragon Herbals

19051 Oaklawn Valley Road
Noble, Oklahoma 73068
www.greendragonherbals.com

Herbal Magick

72 Washington Street
West Warwick, Rhode Island 02893
(401) 826-2573

The Herbal Sage

P.O. Box 1324
Hamlet, North Carolina 28345
(910) 582-0792

Herbalist and Alchemist

P.O. Box 553
Broadway, New Jersey 08808
(908) 689-9020

Herbs and Arts

2015 East Colfax Avenue
Denver, Colorado 80206
(303) 388-2544

Herbs from the Forest

P.O. Box 655
Bearsville, New York 12409

The Hermit's Grove Herb Closet
(by appointment only)
9724 132nd Ave NE
Kirkland, WA 98033
Fax: (425) 803-2025
www.thehermitsgrove.org/pl.html

Joan Teresa Power Products
P.O. Box 442
Mars Hill, North Carolina 28754
(704) 689-5739

Le Sorciere
1281 University Avenue, Suite A
San Diego, California 92103
(619) 29-WITCH

The Magick Cauldron
528 Westheimer Road
Houston, Texas 77006
(877) 622-8587
(713) 523-0069
Fax: (713) 807-0223
www.magickcauldron.com/herbs.htm

Magus Books and Herbs
1316 SE 4th Street
Minneapolis, Minnesota 55414
(612) 379-7669
Fax: (603) 761-4563
www.magusbooks.com/main

Mesmerize
26 Wellgate
Rotherham, South Yorkshire
S60 2LR England
Phone: 01709-821-403
www.mesmerize-uk.com/herbs.html

Moon Maid Botanicals
P.O. Box 182
Sebastopol, California 95473
(707) 586-3971

Moonrise Herbs and Gifts
51420 Highway 60
Wickenburg, Arizona 85390
(520) 684-1077

Mountain Spirit Herbals
P.O. Box 368
Port Townsend, Washington 98368
(800) 817-7233

The Occult Emporium
P.O. Box 5342
Blue Jay, California 92317
(909) 336-1263
www.theoccultemporium.com

Panpipes Magickal Marketplace
1641 Cahuenga Boulevard
Hollywood, California 90028
(323) 462-7078
Fax: (323) 462-6700
http://www.panpipes.com

Papa Jim's Botanica

5630 South Flores Street
San Antonio, Texas 78214
(210) 922-6665; Fax: (210) 922-8277
www.papajims.com

Points of Light

4358 Stearns Street
Long Beach, California 90815
(562) 985-3388

The Sorcerer's Apprentice

6-8 Burley Lodge Road
Leeds, LS6 1QP
Yorkshire, England
Phone: 0113-245-1309
www.sorcerers-apprentice.co.uk

Wise Woman Center

P.O. Box 64
Woodstock, New York 12498
(845) 246-8081

Wise Woman Herbals

P.O. Box 279
Creswell, Oregon 97426
(800) 476-6518

For additional shops and mail -order businesses that cater to the magickal community, see my book, *The Modern Witches' Complete Source Book* (Kensington/Citadel Press, 2001).

Chapter 13:
Gods and Goddesses

The following is an alphabetically-arranged list of Pagan gods and goddesses from various pantheons throughout the world. Each deity is linked in one way or another to plants, trees, flowers, medicinal herbs, magickal herbs, and the planting and/or harvesting of crops. Invoke one the next time you plant an herb garden, gather wildflowers, or celebrate a harvest rite.

Abellio: Romano-Celtic (Gallic) god of apple trees.

Abnoba: Romano-Celtic (Continental European) goddess of forests and rivers.

Abundantia: Roman goddess of agriculture who personifies abundance.

Agrotes: Phoenician god of agriculture.

Ah Bolon Dz'acab: Mayan god of fertility who is linked with agriculture and young crops. He wears a leaf-like ornament in his nose.

Ahmakiq: Mayan god of agriculture.

Ah Mun: Mayan god of maize. He is said to guard over unripe corn.

Airmid (Airmed): Celtic goddess of healing. As a protectress of medicinal plants, she presided over herbal lore. She is also the keeper of the spring that returns the dead to life.

Aizan: Voodoo loa (deity) of the marketplace and herbal healing. She is also the protectress of the houngan (temple) and religious ceremonies. Unlike other loas, she never possesses devotees during ritual. The palm leaf is her symbol, and white and silver are her sacred colors.

Aja: African forest goddess, worshiped by the Yoruba people. She teaches the medicinal use of herbs to the mortal race.

Akka: Finnish earth mother and goddess of the harvest.

Amaethon: Celtic god of agriculture, ploughing, and husbandry.

Anna Kuari: Indian goddess of vegetation. She was believed to grant plentiful harvests and riches to those who propitiated her with human sacrifices during her springtime rites.

Aralo (Aray): Armenian god of agriculture.

Aranyani: Hindu goddess of woodlands. She is said to be a benign and elusive deity.

Arduinna: Romano-Celtic (Continental European) goddess of forests and hunting. She is identified with the Roman goddess Diana.

Ashnan (Asnan): Sumerian goddess of grain and wheat.

Attis: Phrygian god of vegetation; worshipped from circa 5000 B.C. until circa 400 A.D. According to mythology, he castrated himself beneath a pine tree to offer his vitality to the goddess Cybele. In Rome, where his cult was brought in 204 A.D., his annual festival was celebrated on the 22nd of March-a date later supplanted by the Christians' festival of Easter.

Axo-Mama: South American Indian goddess who presides over the growing and harvesting of potato crops. According to Michael Jordan's *Encyclopedia of Gods,* "A model of this minor deity was made out of parts of the plant as a harvest fetish and kept a year before being burned in a ritual to ensure a good potato harvest."

Azaca: Voodoo loa (deity) of agriculture and a protector of the crops. He is depicted as a peasant man carrying a straw bag. Blue is his sacred color, and cornmeal or corn cakes are sacrificed to him.

Balarama: Hindu god of agriculture and fertility, whose name means "strength of Rama." He is an incarnation of the god Vishnu, and his attributes include the fan palm, lotus, and plough.

Bres Macelatha: Celtic god of vegetation.

Bris: Celtic (Irish) god of fertility and agriculture.

Centeocihuatl (Centeotl): Aztec goddess of corn.

Ceres: Roman goddess of agriculture and corn, who was worshipped at the *Thesmophoria* and *Cerealia* festivals in sanctuaries throughout the Greco-Roman empires. According to Barbara G. Walker in *The Women's Encyclopedia of Myths and Secrets*, "Farmers [both Roman and Christian] viewed her as the source of all food and kept her rites faithfully, for fear of crop failure." Ceres is the Roman version of the Greek goddess Demeter.

"Invocation to Ceres"
Grant us the wisdom to see thy ways in all living things,
Grant us thy fruitful protection!
Grant us the power to heal the land,
Grant us thy fruitful protection!
O beautiful Ceres and Great Mother Isis are One!
Grant us thy fruitful protection!
—Psyche in Apuleisus

Cerridwen: Celtic goddess of inspiration who also presided over herbs, grains, and potions. According to mythology, she is the keeper of the cauldron of knowledge and a deity who transforms into a white, corpse-eating sow. Some historians believe that her cult may have originated thousands of years ago on the island of Malta, where archeologists had discovered prehistoric temples bearing images of a sacred sow-goddess.

Chac: Aztec god of plants and rain.

Chalchiuhtlicue: Aztec water goddess; particularly invoked as a guardian goddess of young women. According to Michael Jordan's *Encyclopedia of Gods*, "She takes the role of a vegetation goddess responsible for the flowering and fruiting of the green world, particularly corn."

Chicomecohuatl: Aztec goddess of corn, whose annual September festival called for the gruesome sacrifice of a young girl by means of decapitation on a heap of corn fruits. After being collected in a wooden bowl, the girl's blood would be poured over a wooden figurine of the goddess; her skin would then be flayed off and worn by a dancing priest.

Chloris: Greek goddess of flowers, and counterpart to the Roman goddess Flora.

Cinteotl: Aztec god of maize.

Coca-Mama: Peruvian goddess of the coca plant. To ensure a good coca harvest, the Indians of South America are said to have fashioned the leaves of coca plants into small figures that represented the goddess. These figures (similar in appearance and function to the corn-dollies used by European pagans) would be kept for a period of one year and then ritually burned.

Consus: Roman god of agriculture.

Dagon (Dagan): Mesopotamian (Babylonian-Akkadian) god of grain and fertility.

Demeter: Greek vegetation and mother goddess, who was also a deity connected to death and the underworld. Her cult was widespread and often practiced in secrecy with initiation rites. Some sources claim that the sacrificing of young virgins was carried out during Demeter's annual festivals to ensure fertility;

 however, not enough historical evidence exists to substantiate this. Like many pagan deities, Demeter is a goddess known by many different names-one of them being the Barley-Mother. In *The Women's Encyclopedia of Myths and Secrets*, Barbara G. Walker states, "Rustics never ceased believing that Demeter's spirit was manifest in the final sheaf of the harvest..." This would explain why such sheaves were often known as the Demeter, the Corn Mother, the Old Woman, and other similar names.

Dosojin: Japanese Shinto god who protects the roads and travelers. His sacred symbol is the phallus, and he presides over agriculture, fertility, and procreation. Farmers invoked him to ensure an abundant harvest.

Dumuzi: Sumerian god of vegetation and the underworld, and a deity particularly associated with date palms and their harvest. According to ancient mythology, Dumuzi is required to dwell in the underworld for a portion of each year before being rescued by his consort, the goddess Inanna. His absence is thus responsible for the "seasonal demise of the green world to drought."

Dxui: African creator god who took the form of a different flower or plant each day, changing back into his original form nightly, until he had created all of the flowers and plants that exist on earth.

Egres (Akras): Karelian (Finland) god of fertility. He is invoked by farmers of turnip crops.

Eir: Nordic goddess of healing and a consort of the god Frigg. She taught the art of healing and revealed the secret powers of herbs only to women, said to be the only physicians in ancient Scandinavia.

Emutet: Egyptian cobra-headed goddess of agriculture and the harvest.

Enbilulu: Mesopotamian (Sumerian and Babylonian-Akkadian) god of agriculture. According to mythology, the creator god Enki placed Enbilulu in charge of the sacred rivers Tigris and Euphrates.

Eshara: Chaldean goddess of agriculture.

Fauna: Roman goddess of vegetation. She is the consort of the god Faunus, and a guardian of forests and plants.

Faunus: Roman god of vegetation. He is the consort of the goddess Fauna, and a guardian of forests and plants. Faunus possesses many of the same attributes as the god Pan, including goat-like horns and legs.

Felicitas: Roman god associated with agricultural prosperity.

Flora: Roman goddess of gardens, flowers, and blooming plants. In works of art, she is often shown wearing a wreath of springtime flowers in her hair. She was mainly worshiped by young girls, who would lay offerings of fruit and flowers upon her altar. Her annual festival, the *Floralia*, was celebrated from the 28th of April to early May.

Fornax: Roman goddess of grain.

Freya (Freyja): Nordic (Icelandic) or Germanic goddess of fertility and vegetation. Her role was also that of a love goddess

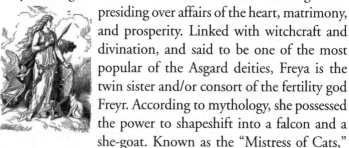

presiding over affairs of the heart, matrimony, and prosperity. Linked with witchcraft and divination, and said to be one of the most popular of the Asgard deities, Freya is the twin sister and/or consort of the fertility god Freyr. According to mythology, she possessed the power to shapeshift into a falcon and a she-goat. Known as the "Mistress of Cats," she rode across the sky in a chariot drawn by two great cats. The centers of her cult were located mainly in Norway and

Sweden, but spread throughout the Nordic region. Friday ("Freya Day") is said to be "the luckiest day for weddings" because it was sacred to Freya.

Invocation to Freya

Leader of the Wind Riders,

You who weaves fates and destinies

and before Whose magick men and Gods do bow,

I call to thee, Freya, Goddess of Power!

Blessed Queen of the shining Realms,

Lady of Folkvang, Sorceress most adept

I call to thee, Freya, to join my Circle!

Leader of the Valkyries,

You who rules half of all Valhalla

and who holds the Necklace of Enchantment,

I pray You come to my call!

Hail to Freya, Queen of Heaven!

Shining Warrior of the Vanir

Keeper of the Mysteries ,

and Prophetess of All Times

Hail and welcome!

Hail and welcome!

—Adapted from *The Rites of Odin*, by Ed Fitch.

Fu-His: Chinese god of agriculture and vegetation. He is also said to be the inventor of writing.

Gabjauja: Lithuanian goddess of grain. After Christianity supplanted Paganism in Lithuania, the role of Gabjauja was transformed from a benevolent goddess into an evil demon.

Ganaskidi: Native American (Navaho) god of harvests, plenty, and of mists. According to legend, he resides in a canyon called Depehahatil.

Geb: Egyptian god of vegetation and the earth. He is also said to be a god of healing, and was frequently invoked by the ancient Egyptians for protection against scorpion stings. In works of art, he is depicted as a green-colored man with greenery sprouting forth from his body.

Gefjon (Gefiun): Germanic and Nordic (Icelandic) goddess of vegetation, agriculture, and fertility. She is a shapeshifter who symbolizes growth, prosperity, virginity, good fortune, and the magickal arts. According to mythology, she gave birth to four giant sons whom she transformed into oxen and used for ploughing the land. One of the Aesir deities, she is said to have been the founder of a royal Danish dynasty. Legend has it that maidens who died as virgins became her servants. Gefjon's symbol is the plough.

Grand Bois: Voodoo loa (deity) of the forest.

Gucumatz: Mayan god of farming, agriculture, civilization, and all matters of a domestic nature. According to mythology, he dwelled in heaven and hell at the same time.

Halki: Hittite and Hurrian god of barley and corn. It is believed that he was invoked by beer makers.

Haumiatiketike: Polynesian god of vegetation; concerned with wild plants gathered as food. His sacred plant is the bracken.

Hegemone: Greek goddess of the soil.

Hiisi: Karelian (Finland) god of trees. It is said he resides in pine forests. After the advent of Christianity, those of the "new religion" reduced him from a god to a troll.

Hou-chi: Chinese god of harvest and agriculture. In works of art, he is depicted as a kindly old man with stalks growing from the top of his head.

Hsien Nung: Chinese god of agriculture.

Hsien Se: Chinese god of agriculture.

Hun Nal: Mayan god of maize.

Ialonus: Romano-Celtic god of meadows.

Imporcitor: Roman god of agriculture, concerned with the harrowing of fields.

Inari: Shinto god or goddess of rice, whose name means "rice grower." Inari, who possesses many personalities and can be either male or female, is revered throughout Japan.

Insitor: Roman god of agriculture, concerned with the sowing of crops.

Itzam Na: Mayan god of creation, whose aspects include a vegetation god, a fire god, and a god of medicine. In ancient carvings he is shown having a long branching nose shaped like two infolded leaves.

Iyatiku: Native American (Pueblo) goddess of corn and ruler of the underground realm to where the dead cross over. In addition to agriculture and a good harvest, she symbolizes death, compassion, sympathy, and children.

Kaikara: Ugandan harvest goddess.

Kaya-Nu-Hima: Japanese goddess of herbs.

Kondos: Finnish god of wheat and sowing.

Kornjunfer: Germanic goddess of corn.

Kouretes: Greek forest deities, said to be the spirits of trees and streams.

Kronos: Greek god of fertility, agriculture, and seeds.

Krumine: Lithuanian god of corn.

Kuku-Toshi-No-Kami: Japanese (Shinto) god of rice and harvest.

Kupala: Slavic goddess of trees, flowers, and herbal lore. Purple loosestrife and ferns are her most sacred plants. According to an old legend, the fern opens its "fire-flowers" on the eve of the Summer Solstice (known as the "Eve of Kupala") and anyone who possesses this flower will gain the power to read the thoughts of others, to find hidden treasure, to understand the secret language of trees, and to repel all evils.

Lactanus: Roman god of agriculture.

Lai Cho: Chinese god of agriculture.

Lauka Mate: Latvian goddess of agriculture. To ensure a good crop, farmers would invoke her in the fields at ploughing time.

Liu Meng Chiang-Chun: Chinese god of agriculture.

Loko (Loco): African god of vegetation, who is often worshipped in the form of a tree. It is said that he knows the secret properties of all herbs. Loko is often called upon for agricultural needs, such as plant growth. Herbalists invoke him prior to obtaining medicines from the bark and leaves of forest trees.

Lono: Polynesian god who presided over agriculture. In Hawaii, he was one aspect of a triple god figure that also included Kane (the lord of light) and Ku (the lord of stability).

Lupercus: Roman god of wolves, who also presided over agriculture. His annual festival, the *Lupercalia*, was celebrated on the 15th of February.

Malakbel: Arabian god of vegetation.

Mang Shen: Chinese god of agriculture.

Marica: Roman goddess of agriculture.

Medeine: Latvian goddess of the woodlands. Her name means, "of the trees."

Messor: Roman god of agriculture. He presided over the growth and harvesting of crops.

Miao Hu: Chinese god of agriculture.

Mi-Toshi-No-Kami: Japanese (Shinto) god of agriculture, and the son of O-Toshi-No-Kami (god of the rice harvest).

Myrrha: Phoenician goddess of the myrrh tree.

Nanan-Bouclou: Original god of the Ewe tribe (Africa). In Haiti, he was worshiped as the god of herbs and medicines, and invoked during healing rituals.

Nanna: Nordic (Icelandic) goddess of plants and flowers.

Nefertum: Egyptian god who is the blue lotus blossom of Ra.

Nemetona: Romano-Celtic goddess of sacred groves.

Neper: Egyptian god of grain crops, and the son of the snake spirit Renenutet. Like Osiris, he is also a vegetation deity who dies and is reborn to the afterlife.

Nepit: Egyptian goddess of corn.

Ningal: Mesopotamian (Sumerian and Babylonian-Akkadian) goddess of reeds.

Ningikuga: Mesopotamian (Sumerian and Babylonian-Akkadian) goddess of reeds and marshlands. Her name means, "lady of the pure reed."

Ninlil: Mesopotamian (Sumerian) goddess of the air and of grain. According to mythology, she is the daughter of the god Haia and the barley goddess Ninsebargunnu.

Nin-sar: Mesopotamian (Sumerian) mother goddess whose name means "lady plant."

Ninurta: Mesopotamian (Sumerian and Babylonian-Akkadian) god of thunderstorms and the plough. The creator of mountains, and a hero of the Sumerian pantheon who battles against the forces of evil, Ninurta was the patron deity of farmers during his period of worship (circa 3500 B.C. to 200 B.C.)

Obarator: Roman god of agriculture, who presides over the fertilizing of crops.

Occator: Roman god of agriculture, who oversees the growth and harvesting of crops.

Oko: Yoruba (Nigeria, West Africa) god of cultivated land, the harvest, and plenty. His name means "hoe," and his festival, which emphasizes fertility, is held each year at the start of the rainy season. In the Santeria tradition, he is an orisha (deity) of fertility and a judge of the orisha. Whenever a dispute arises between them, he is the one who settles it. Women who desire children invoke him to ensure fertility.

Onatha: Native American (Iroquois) goddess of wheat.

Ops (Ops Runcina): Roman goddess of agriculture, harvest, fertility, abundance, childbirth, and prosperity. She regulated the proper growth of seeds and was invoked by touching the earth. Her annual festival was celebrated on the 25th day of August.

Osain: In the Santeria tradition, Osain is the orisha (deity) of the trees and plants that grow wild in the rainforest. Yellow, red, and white are his sacred colors, and Sunday is the day of the week sacred to him. He is said to be a great herbalist, and offerings must be presented to him before any of his plants may be gathered. According to legend, he ruled over all healing plants, which he kept safe in his calabash gourd hung high in a tree. The other orishas were jealous of his herbal wisdom and summoned up a fierce wind to blow the calabash out of the tree. They then snatched up as many of the fallen plants as they could for themselves. Osain grants the knowledge of medical and magickal uses of herbs to devotees who present him with sacrificial offerings. He is a *brujo* (a male witch) and his powers of magick are great. It is said that he grew from the soil of the earth like a plant.

Osiris: Egyptian lord of the underworld, who also took on the

role of a deity concerned with grain and vegetation. In the *Encyclopedia of Gods*, it is said, "As a grain god, Osiris was worshiped in the form of a sack filled with seed that sprouted green." His annual death and re-birth personified the self-renewing vitality and fertility of nature.

"Invocation of Osiris"

I am Osiris Onnophris who is found perfect before the Gods.

I hath said: These are the elements of my Body

perfected through suffering, glorified through trial.

The scent of the dying Rose is as the repressed sigh of my Suffering.

And the flame-red Fire as the energy of mine undaunted Will.

And the Cup of Wine is the pouring out of the blood of my heart,

sacrificed unto Regeneration, unto the newer life.

And the bread and salt are as the foundations of my body,

which I destroy in order that they may be renewed.

For I am Osiris Triumphant. Even Osiris Onnophris the Justified One.

I am He who is clothed with the body of flesh

yet in whom flames the spirit of the eternal Gods.

I am the Lord of Life. I am triumphant over Death,

and whosoever partaketh with me shall with me arise.

I am the manifester in Matter of Those whose abode is the Invisible.

I am the purified. I stand upon the Universe.

I am it's Reconciler with the eternal Gods.

I am the Perfector of Matter, and without me the Universe is not."

Pai Chung: Chinese god of agriculture.

Patrimpas: Lithuanian god of agriculture.

Pekko: Finnish and Baltic god of cereal crops. In Finland, he was worshiped as the god of barley, and was invoked as a patron deity by brewers of beer.

Pellervoinen: Finnish god of trees, plants, and fields.

Pellon Pekko: Finnish vegetation god who presides over the germination and harvesting of the barley used to make beer.

Picus: Roman god of agriculture.

Pitao Cozobi: Zapotec (Mexico) god of corn.

Pomona: Roman goddess of orchards and gardens, who symbolized all fruition and to whom all fruit trees were sacred. According to Barbara G. Walker, every banquet of the ancient Romans ended with the eating of apples, "as an invocation of Pomona's good will." Pomona's festival, the *Pomonalia*, was celebrated every year in pre-Christian Rome on November 1st to mark the completion of the harvest.

Promitor: Roman god of agriculture, who presides over the growth and harvesting of crops.

Proserpina: Roman goddess of the underworld. The Roman equivalent of the Greek goddess Persephone, Proserpina is also a deity who presides over the germination of seeds.

Puta: Roman goddess of agriculture. She presides over the pruning of trees and shrubs.

Quinoa-Mama: Peruvian goddess of quinoa plant, invoked to ensure a good quinine harvest.

Ranno: Egyptian god of gardens.

Redarator: Roman god of agriculture. He was invoked by sacrificial rites, which the ancients believed were essential to the welfare of their crops.

Renenutet (Renenet): Egyptian snake and fertility goddess. Farmers throughout the fertile region of the Nile valley invoked her name to ensure good crops and harvests.

Robigo: Roman goddess of grain. Her name means "mildew," and she was invoked by farmers to protect the wheat crops from mildew during damp seasons.

Robigus: Roman god of corn and grain.

Rongomatane: Polynesian god of agriculture and the father of cultivated food. The *kumara* (sweet potato) is sacred to him.

Sabazios: Phrygian god of agriculture.

Saning Sari: Javan goddess of the rice plant. She is known as the "rice mother."

Sanju: Kafir harvest goddess who was worshipped in Afghanistan in the form of a human or a goat. She presided over the harvesting, threshing, and winnowing of grain, and it is said that the blood of sacrificial animals poured upon her wooden statue invoked her.

Sarritor: Roman god of agriculture. Farmers would invoke him during the planting and harvesting of crops.

Saturn: Roman astral god, originally worshipped as an agricultural and harvest deity concerned with the sowing of seed. His annual festival, the *Saturnalia*, was celebrated in ancient Rome from the 17th to the 19th of December.

Satyrs: Greco-Roman woodland gods. They appear as part human and part goat, and are said to be extremely lusty by nature.

Semargl: Slavic god of barley.

Serapis: Egyptian god of corn and grain.

Shang Ti (Shang Di, Yu Huang Shang Ti): Chinese god of agriculture.

She Chi: Chinese god of agriculture, grain, and soil.

Shen Nung: Chinese god of agriculture, pharmacy, and health; known as "the divine farmer." Said to be the inventor of the plough, he instructed humans in basic agriculture and in the magickal, medicinal, and culinary use of herbs. He symbolizes the element of air.

Shui Fang: Chinese god of agriculture.

Shui Yng: Chinese god of agriculture.

Si: Peruvian moon god who presided over harvests and the weather. He was worshiped by the Chimu Indians.

Sif: Nordic (Icelandic) and Germanic goddess of grain, and the consort of the mighty god Thor. According to some sources, she was originally a golden-haired prophetess named Sibyl.

Silvanus: Roman god of forests and woodlands, whose sacred animal is the stag.

Spiniensis: Roman god of agriculture, who presides over the uprooting of thorny bushes.

Ssu Cho: Chinese god of agriculture.

Sterculius: Roman god of agriculture, who presides over the manuring of the fields.

Sucellus: Romano-Celtic god of agriculture and forests, worshiped from prehistoric times until the advent of Christianity. According to mythology, he ferries souls to the underworld. His consort is the river goddess Nantosuelta.

Sylvanus: Roman god of woodlands, fields, and herding, depicted in ancient works of art as a bearded satyr.

Tammuz: Assyrian god of agriculture.

Tane (Tanemahuta): Polynesian god of light, trees, and forests. He is known as Kane in the Hawaiian Islands, and patron god of boat builders. According to mythology, he descends to the underworld every evening to join his consort (or, in other traditions, his sister) who reigns as the goddess of death.

Ta-No-Kami: A generic name for several Shinto (Japanese) agricultural deities who preside over crops and harvests.

Telipinu: Hittite and Hurrian god of vegetation and fertility. Each year, Telipinu disappears and is rediscovered to symbolize the annual "death" and "rebirth" cycle of nature. It was customary for those who worshiped him to fill a hollow tree trunk with harvest offerings.

Tellus: Roman goddess of grain. She was generally regarded as a benevolent deity, although one of her aspects was a goddess of the dead. The Romans propitiated her with human sacrifice, offering enemy armies to her and cursing them in her name.

Tulsi: Indian goddess of basil plants.

Ua-Ildak: Mesopotamian (Babylonian-Akkadian) goddess of vegetation. She was a guardian of pastures and poplar trees.

Ubertas: Roman god of agriculture. He was often invoked for prosperity.

Ugar: Syrian god of vegetation.

Uwolowu: African sky god and creator of all things, including the minor gods. He is a beneficent deity, who is said to have given fire to mankind. He presides over agriculture, harvests, spring, birth, rain, and the sun.

Vacuna: Roman goddess of agriculture.

Vertumnus: Roman god of gardens and orchards, to whom offerings of fruits and flowers would be made. Like his consort, the goddess Pomona, he was generally represented by garden implements. His festival, the *Vertumnalia*, was celebrated each year on the 13th of August.

Waka-Sa-Na-Me-No-Kami: Japanese (Shinto) goddess of agriculture who presides over the transplanting of young rice plants.

Waka-Toshi-No-Kami: Japanese (Shinto) god of agriculture who presides over the growing of young rice plants.

Xilonen: Aztec goddess of vegetation. She was an aspect of the corn goddess Chicomecoatl, and a personification of the corn plant.

Xipe Totec: Aztec god of agriculture, plants, and seeds, who symbolized the annual renewal of vegetation. Xipe Totec was a significant deity of the Mesoamerican pantheons. According to the *Encyclopedia of Gods*, he was "Often represented in ritual by a priest wearing the flayed skin of a human sacrifice, seen to be the new vegetation of the earth that emerges after the rains." The skin would be worn for a period of three weeks.

Xochipilli: Aztec god of maize.

Xochiquetzal-Ichpuchtli: Aztec fertility goddess associated with flowers, erotic love, and pleasure.

Yaksas: Hindu tree spirits.

Yanauluha: Native American (Zuni) god known as the "great medicine man." He symbolizes agriculture, animal husbandry, healing, knowledge, and society.

Yobin-Pogil: Siberian forest deity (or spirit) who guards over the woodlands.

Yolkai Estan: Native American (Navajo) earth goddess of the four seasons and the land. Her name means "White Shell Woman." She was invoked for fertility as well as for agriculture.

Yum Kaax: Mayan god of vegetation, who presides over the growing and harvesting of corn (as well as husbandry in general). In works of art, he is depicted as a young man wearing a headdress containing an ear of corn.

Zaka: Voodoo god of agriculture.

Zara-Mama: Peruvian goddess of corn.

Zemepatis: Lithuanian god who watches over cattle. In pre-Christian times, he was the patron deity of all men who farmed the land.

Zisa: German goddess of harvests.

Appendix: A Calendar of Magickal Herb Lore

January

5th: On the eve before the Festival of the Three Kings, an old Christian tradition calls for blessed dried herbs to be ritually burned and doorways sprinkled with holy water.

6th: Twelfth Day. According to a centuries-old English tradition, all yuletide decorations of holly, ivy, mistletoe, and evergreens should be removed from the house and burnt on the morning of Twelfth Day (the last day of the yuletide season). This is believed to avert 12 months of bad luck or a death in the family.

13th: In some parts of the world, the old Pagan custom of wassailing apple trees each year on this day continues to be observed.

20th: Saint Agnes' Eve: According to Pagan tradition, drinking parsley tea and eating stale bread before going to sleep this night will bring you a dream about the man or woman destined to be your future marriage partner. The Celtic tree month of Birch (Beth) ends.

21st: The Celtic tree month of Rowan (Luis) begins.

February

2nd: Candlemas (also known as Imbolc), one of the four major sabbats celebrated each year by Witches and other Pagans, is observed on this day. The traditional herbs associated with this sabbat include: angelica, basil, bay, myrrh, celandine, heather, wisteria, and all yellow flowers.

3rd: On this day the Japanese celebrate their annual *Setsu-bun* festival, during which people drive away evil spirits by throwing dried soy beans (one for each year of their age) and chanting: *"Oni-wa soto! Fuku-wa uchi!"* (Translation: "Devils out! Good luck in!")

8th: Birthday of herbalist and author, Susun Weed.

13th: Herbal lore holds that if a young woman sleeps this night with five bay leaves beneath her pillow, she will dream about the man destined to be her future husband. If she does not dream, this is said to be an omen that she will remain a spinster for at least another year.

14th: Saint Valentine's Day. In the Victorian language of flowers, the following plants speak of love in the following ways: ambrosia (love returned), bridal rose (marriage), coreopsis (love at first sight), forget-me-not (true love, forget me not), ivy (marriage and fidelity), lemon blossom (fidelity in love), linden (conjugal love), lotus flower (estranged love), moss (maternal love), motherwort (concealed love), myrtle (love), pink carnation (woman's love), rose (love), yellow acacia (secret love), yellow tulip (hopeless love).

17th: In ancient Rome, an annual festival known as the *Fornacalia* was observed to pay homage to the oven goddess and to ensure a good growing season for crops. "On this day," says Nigel Pennick in *The Pagan Book of Days*, "plants should be tended with extra loving care." The Celtic tree month of Rowan (Luis) ends.

18th: The Celtic tree month of Ash (Nuin) begins.

23rd: The maple tree and its sugar are honored on this day by the Iroquois Indians.

24th: In Elizabethan times, bridesmaids traditionally planted sprigs of myrtle each year on this day to make their romances blossom into marriage.

March

1st: Saint David's Day honors the patron saint of Wales and his sacred plants, the leek and the daffodil, which symbolize vigorous growth.

14th: The Runic half-month of Boerc, which is symbolized by the birch tree, begins on this day.

16th: In ancient Greece, the annual 2-day rites of Dionysus began on this day to honor the wine-god and to ensure a bountiful grape harvest.

17th: Saint Patrick's Day is observed each year on this day. It is said that Saint Patrick is actually an assimilation of the Pagan Celtic deity Trefuilngid Tre-eochair, whose sacred plant, the shamrock, bore all edible fruits including the apples of immortality. This day marks the rebirth of the Green Man (a deity who embodies the vitality of all plant life). In olden times, an annual festival for the greening of Mother Earth was celebrated on this day in Europe. The Celtic tree month of Ash (Nuin) ends.

18th: The Celtic tree month of Alder (Fearn) begins.

19th: On this day, the annual Yoruba and Santeria feast in honor of Osanyin, the Orisha of Green Leaves, is celebrated.

21st: The Spring Equinox, one of the four minor (or lesser) sabbats observed by Witches and other Pagans, occurs approximately on this date each year. The traditional herbs associated with this sabbat include: acorns, celandine, cinquefoil, crocus, daffodil, dogwood, Easter lily, honeysuckle, iris, jasmine, rose, strawberry, tansy, and violets.

April

10th: On this day in the year 1872, residents of the state of Nebraska planted close to one million trees in celebration of the first Arbor Day. (In 1882, Nebraska declared Arbor Day a legal holiday and changed its date to April 22, which was J. Sterling Morton's birthday.) Throughout most of the United States, Arbor Day is currently observed each year on the last Friday in April —a day on which many Wiccans and Pagans plant trees, perform special tree-honoring rituals, meditate on Deity manifesting as trees, and give thanks for the abundance of the earth.

12th: The first day of the annual 8-day *Cerealia* festival was celebrated in ancient Rome on this day. It paid homage to the goddess Ceres, who was connected to the earth and its fruits, and included sacred rites to guard the crops against failure.

14th: The Celtic tree month of Alder (Fearn) ends.

15th: The Celtic tree month of Willow (Saille) begins.

16th: In the Middle Ages, Saint Padarn's Day (Celtic) was the traditional time for farmers to begin weeding the growing crops.

22nd: Earth Day. (The first Earth Day was held in the United States in 1970 to raise public awareness of environmental issues and ecology. Twenty years later in 1990, 20 million Americans observed the second Earth Day. Since then it has been observed every year.) On this day, many Wiccans and Pagans throughout the world meditate on Deity manifesting as Mother Earth and perform special rituals to honor her and to heal her from the ravages of mankind.

23rd: This day starts the annual Iroquois planting ceremonies and thanksgiving for the gift of the corn seed.

25th: On this day the ancient Romans celebrated the annual *Robigalia* festival to honor and appease the dual-gendered deity Robigus. Sacrificial offerings of red dogs and sheep were made to prevent blight from the growing grain.

Saint Mark's Day divination: Pluck nine sage leaves as the clock strikes 12 at noon and, according to old herbal lore, your future husband (or a vision of him) will appear before you.

28th: The *Floralia*, an annual 3-day festival honoring the flower-goddess Flora, began on this day in ancient Rome. In ancient and medieval Europe, various vegetation festivals were celebrated every year on this day.

30th: Walpurgis Night. According to medieval legend, this is a night given over to demonic forces and evil spirits. For protection, wear or carry angelica, garlic, mandrake root, rowan, or Saint John's wort as an herbal amulet. On this night, the Horned God of the ancient Celtic and Teutonic peoples was honored. In his Green Man aspect, he personified the spirit of all trees and plants.

May

1st: Beltane, one of the four major sabbats celebrated each year by Witches and other Pagans, is observed on this day. The traditional herbs associated with this sabbat include: almond, angelica, ash tree, bluebells, cinquefoil, daisy, frankincense, hawthorn, ivy, lilac, marigold, meadowsweet, primrose, roses, satyrion root, woodruff, and yellow cowslips. The Pueblo and Zuni Indians of the American southwest celebrate the annual Green Corn Dances on this day. According to legend, the Corn Maidens return to earth at this time to bless and make fruitful the land after the barrenness of the winter season.

3rd: Rowan Tree Day. It is traditional for many Witches and Pagans on this day to gather rowan twigs and leaves for magickal spells and amulets. Decorate your altar and home with sprigs of rowan to court the blessings and protection of the Goddess and Her horned consort. Fires made of rowan wood are believed on this day to possess the power to summon spirits.

4th: The hawthorn (a tree sacred to the "good goddess" Bona Dea and linked to Witches and fairy-folk) is honored on this day. An annual 4-day Iroquois corn-planting ceremony begins on this day and pays homage to the sky goddess Awenhai.

12th: The Celtic tree month of Willow (Saille) ends.

13th: The Celtic tree month of Hawthorn (Huath) begins.

19th: In olden times, the Celtic goddess Brigid was honored on this day by the festival of the Sacred Spring. It was traditional for sacred wells and springs to be decorated with flowers and greenery.

23rd: A sacred rose festival known as the *Rosalia* was celebrated each year on this day in ancient Rome. It honored the flower-goddess Flora.

24th: For prosperity and to ensure a good harvest, every year on this day the ancient Celts would pay homage to the three goddesses known as the Mothers.

25th: On this day of the year, the Iroquois Indians give thanks for the strawberry harvest.

29th: Oak Apple Day. In England, it is customary to wear oak leaves for the first half of the day. In ancient Rome, the *Ambarvalia* festival was held each year on this day to honor Ceres and the Dea Dia, as well as to receive divine blessings for the growing crops.

June

1st: In Celtic cultures, the Festival of the Oak Nymph was celebrated annually on this day to pay homage to the benevolent nature spirits who dwelled within all oak trees.

9th: The Celtic tree month of Hawthorn (Huath) ends.

10th: The Celtic tree month of Oak (Duir) begins.

15th: The ancient Romans observed the *Vestalia*, an annual women's festival celebrating the first fruits of the early harvest season, on this day.

20th: On this day in the year 1889, the first Arbor Day in Australia was celebrated in Adelaide.

21st: The Summer Solstice, one of the four minor (or lesser) sabbats observed by Witches and other Pagans, occurs approximately on this date each year. The traditional herbs associated with this sabbat include: chamomile, cinquefoil, elder, fennel, hemp, larkspur, lavender, male fern, mugwort, pine, roses, Saint John's wort, wild thyme, wisteria, and verbena.

23rd: Saint John's Eve (also known as Midsummer's Eve in many old calendars) is the traditional time for many Witches to gather herbs for amatory spells and philters (love potions). This is also said to be the prime time to harvest Saint John's wort for use in treating individuals suffering from depression and madness of the mind.

24th: Saint John's Day (also known as Midsummer's Day in many old calendars). This is said to be the best day of the year on which to gather vervain for use in love potions. In keeping with an old Pagan tradition, use a gold coin or a stag's horn to dig the plant up. Legend holds that the magickal energies of herbs are at their peak on this day. In the Middle Ages, Saint John's wort is traditionally burned on this day to repel evil spirits and sorcery.

29th: In the English region of East Anglia, those who continue to follow the ancient ways believe that this is the prime day of the year to harvest herbs for healing use. In the English village of Appleton, a centuries-old Pagan tree-worship ritual known as "Bawming the Thorn" takes place each year on this day. Celebrants hang flowers and garlands from the boughs of an ancient hawthorn tree.

July

3rd: On this day the Cherokee Indians (and other Native American tribes) begin celebrating their annual Green Corn Dance festival to honor the maize goddess Selu and to give thanks for the maize harvest.

7th: Consus, the Roman god of harvests, was commemorated on this day by an annual festival known as the *Consualia*. The Celtic tree month of Oak (Duir) ends.

8th: Juno Caprotina, the goddess of the fig tree, was venerated on this day by the annual *Caprotina* festival. Feasts beneath fig trees were held in her honor. The Celtic tree month of Holly (Tinne) begins.

11th: Theano, wife of Pythagoras and the "patroness of vegetarianism," is honored on this day.

12th: On this day the Iroquois Nations begin celebrating their annual Green Bean festival to give thanks for the bean harvest.

14th: On this day in the year 1988, the first appearance of crop circles on Silbury Hill in England was recorded.

15th: Rowana, the goddess of the rowan tree, was honored on this day by the Norse. The magickal powers of rowan trees are believed by some to be the greatest on this day, which is the reason many Witches and Pagan folk traditionally make protective amulets from rowan wood at this time.

August

1st: Lammas (also known as Lughnasadh), one of the four major sabbats celebrated each year by Witches and other Pagans, is observed on this day. The traditional herbs associated with this sabbat include: acacia flowers, aloes, cornstalks, cyclamen, fenugreek, frankincense, heather, hollyhock, myrtle, oak, sunflower, and wheat. As a thanksgiving offering to the Goddess, many Wiccans bake a loaf of corn bread and lay it upon their altar.

4th: The Celtic tree month of Holly (Tinne) ends.

5th: The Celtic tree month of Hazel (Coll) begins.

7th: Gaia Consciousness Day honors Mother Earth in ceremonies of healing and renewal. On this day many Pagans throughout the world meditate upon the Earth as a living entity.

13th: Sleeping with 13 leaves from an ash tree beneath your pillow this night is said to induce dreams of a prophetic nature.

19th: The ancient Romans celebrated the *Rustic Vinalia* festival each year on this day to celebrate the grape harvest and to honor Venus in her aspect as a goddess of the grape vine.

20th: On this day in the year 1937, the U.S. House of Representatives approved the "Marihuana Tax Act" after engaging in only 90 seconds of debate.

23rd: Vertumnus, the ancient Roman god responsible for changing the seasons and transforming flowers into fruits, was honored on this day by an annual festival known as the *Vertumnalia*.

25th: Ops, the ancient Roman goddess who presided over sowing and reaping, was honored on this day by an annual festival known as the *Opiconsivia*.

27th: Legend holds that every year on this day, the anniversary of Saint John the Baptist's death by beheading, red spots mysteriously appear on the leaves of the Saint John's wort plant to symbolize the saint's spilled blood.

September

1st: The Celtic tree month of Hazel (Coll) ends.

2nd: The Celtic tree month of Vine (Muin) begins.

14th: According to folklore from the Middle Ages, every year on this day the Devil roams the forests in search of nuts.

22nd: The Autumn Equinox, one of the four minor (or lesser) sabbats observed by Witches and other Pagans, occurs approximately on this date each year. The traditional herbs associated with this sabbat include: acorns, asters, ferns, honeysuckle, marigold, milkweed, mums, myrrh, oak, passionflower, pine, roses, sage, Solomon's seal, and thistles.

29th: The Celtic tree month of Vine (Muin) ends.

30th: The Celtic tree month of Ivy (Gort) begins.

October

1st: On this day in the year 1937, the "Marihuana Tax Act" took effect, thus beginning the prohibition of marijuana that remains in place today.

11th: According to a centuries-old legend, bad luck will befall anyone who picks or eats blackberries on this day.

12th: Ameretat (one of the seven emanations of God, said to be the creator and guardian of plants) is honored on this day through the 16th by those who follow the Zoroastrian tradition.

18th: On this day in the year 1616, astrologer and herbalist Nicholas Culpepper was born.

22nd: The annual Day of the Willows festival was celebrated on this day in the ancient Babylonian calendar.

27th: The annual Feast of Osiris at Abydos is observed on this day, paying homage to the Neter of vegetation and offering thanks to him for all fruits of the earth. The Celtic tree month of Ivy (Gort) ends.

28th: The Celtic tree month of Reed (Ngetal) begins.

31st: Halloween/Samhain Eve. The old Halloween custom of placing a lit candle inside a hollowed-out pumpkin was at one time believed to ward off demons and evil spirits who walked the earth on this night. Sleeping with an apple beneath the pillow on Halloween night is an old Pagan method to induce prophetic dreams of a future marriage mate. Other Halloween divinations involving plants include the throwing of nuts into a fire to determine the faithfulness of one's lover, the tossing of hemp seeds over one's left shoulder in a churchyard while reciting a special incantation to make a vision of one's future spouse appear, and the uprooting of a cabbage plant while blindfolded to discover the physical attributes, personality, and profession of one's husband-to-be.

November

1st: Samhain, one of the four major sabbats celebrated each year by Witches and other Pagans, is observed on this day. The traditional herbs associated with this sabbat include: acorns, apples, broom, deadly nightshade, dittany of Crete, ferns, flax, fumitory, heather, heliotrope, mandrake, mint, mullein, oak, sage, and straw.

11th: In Ireland, the annual *Lunantishees* festival is held on this day to honor the spirits that inhabit and watch over blackthorn trees, a plant sacred to the fairy-folk. Irish folklore holds that it is extremely unlucky for millers to grind corn on this day.

12th: This day begins the annual 4-day Buffalo Dances, during which the Pueblo Indians of the American Southwest offer thanks for the harvest.

16th: In the ancient Egyptian calendar, this day marks the start of the spring sowing season.

24th: The Celtic tree month of Reed (Ngetal) ends.

25th: The Celtic tree month of Elder (Ruis) begins.

December

21st: The Winter Solstice, one of the four minor (or lesser) sabbats observed by Witches and other Pagans, occurs approximately on this date each year. The traditional herbs associated with this sabbat include: bay, bayberry, blessed thistle, cedar, chamomile, evergreen, frankincense, holly, ivy, juniper, mistletoe, moss, pine, rosemary, and sage. Centuries ago, the annual Festival of Evergreen Trees (a medieval version of Arbor Day) was celebrated in Europe by the planting of evergreen trees and the hanging of evergreen wreaths, which symbolized eternal life.

22nd: The Celtic tree month of Elder (Ruis) ends.

23rd: In the old Celtic tree calendar, this day is known as "The Secret of the Unhewn Stone." It is the one day of the year not ruled by a tree.

24th: Yule logs are traditionally burned on Christmas Eve to ensure good health and good fortune throughout the coming year. In addition, they symbolize the union of the male and female aspects of the Divine. It is said that to avoid bad luck, holly must be picked before Christmas Eve but not brought into the house prior to this day. The Celtic tree month of Birch (Beth) begins.

25th: The traditional herbs of Christmas include: bayberry, holly, ivy, mistletoe, pine, and poinsettia. Kissing while standing beneath a sprig of mistletoe is traditionally done for good luck. It some parts of England it is believed that cutting mistletoe on any day of the year other than Christmas brings bad luck to one's family and home.

28th: The Runic half-month of Eoh, which is symbolized by the yew tree, begins on this day.

Elemental Magick

Air:

By element of liberation,
Breath of life and transformation,
Winds of change and good vibration,
Bless these words of incantation.

Fire:

Vibrant energies that ignite
Flames of passion burning bright,
Dragon sun of golden light
Empowers with the Horned One's might.

Water:

Secrets of the moon-kissed ocean
Dancing with unending motion,
Witch's cauldron full of potion
Brews a spell charged with emotion.

Earth:

From root and skull to skull and bone,
Pyramid to runes of stone,
Seeds of magick now be sown
And grow for the Maiden,
The Mother, and Crone.

Storm and fire, land and sea,
Enchant this magick rhyme for me.

In perfect love these words are stated
And in perfect trust created.
Now this magick rhyme is done,
This charm is fixed and it harms none.

—from *Priestess and Pentacle*
by Gerina Dunwich

Bibliography

Bremness, Lesley. *Herbs*. New York: Dorling Kindersley, 1994.

Buchman, Dian Dincin. *Herbal Medicine: The Natural Way to Get Well and Stay Well*. New York: Wings Books, 1996.

Budge, E. A. Wallis. *Amulets and Superstitions*. New York: Dover Publications, 1978.

Cavendish, Richard. *The Black Arts*. New York: Perigee Books, 1983.

Cohen, Daniel. *Magicians, Wizards, and Sorcerers*. New York: J.B. Lippincott Company, 1973.

Culbertson, Molly, ed. *Country Home Book of Herbs*. Des Moines, Iowa: Meredith Books, 1994.

Cunningham, Scott. *Cunningham's Encyclopedia of Magical Herbs*. St. Paul, Minnesota: Llewellyn Publications, 1985.

Dunwich, Gerina. *The Wicca Garden*. Secaucus, New Jersey: Citadel Press, 1996.

Dunwich, Gerina. *The Wicca Book of Days*. Secaucus, New Jersey: Citadel Press, 1995.

Fraser, Angus. *The Gypsies*. Oxford, England: Blackwell Publishers, 1992.

Haining, Peter. *The Warlock's Book*. New Hyde Park, New York: University Books, 1976.

Harding, Deborah C. *The Green Guide to Herb Gardening*. St. Paul, Minnesota: Llewellyn Publications, 2000.

Harrar, Sari and Sara Altshul O'Donnell. *The Woman's Book of Healing Herbs*. Emmaus, Pennsylvania: Rodale Press, Inc., 1999.

Harrop, Renny, ed. *Encyclopedia of Herbs*. Secaucus, New Jersey: Chartwell Books, 1977.

Jordan, Michael. *Encyclopedia of Gods*. New York: Facts on File, Inc., 1993.

Leek, Sybil. *Sybil Leek's Book of Herbs*. Nashville, Tennessee: Thomas Nelson, Inc., 1973.

Leland, Charles Godfrey. *Gypsy Sorcery and Fortune Telling*. New Hyde Park, New York: University Books, 1962.

Lucas, Richard. *The Magic of Herbs in Daily Living*. West Nyack, New York: Parker Publishing Company, 1972.

McDowell, Bart. *Gypsies: Wanderers of the World*. Washington, D.C.: The National Geographic Society, 1970.

Ody, Penelope. *The Complete Medicinal Herbal*. New York: Dorling Kindersley, Inc., 1993.

Opie, Iona, and Moira Tatem, editors. *A Dictionary of Superstitions*. New York: Oxford University Press, 1989.

O'Rush, Claire. *The Enchanted Garden*. North Pomfret, Vermont: Trafalgar Square Publishing, 1996.

Pennick, Nigel. *The Pagan Book of Days*. Rochester, Vermont: Destiny Books, 1992.

Pickering, David. *Dictionary of Superstitions*. London: Cassell, 1995.

Reader's Digest. *Magic and Medicine of Plants*. Pleasantville, New York: The Reader's Digest Association, 1986.

Sanecki, Kay N. *The Complete Book of Herbs*. New York: Macmillan Publishing Company, 1974.

Shaw, Eva. *Divining the Future*. New York: Facts on File, 1995.

Walker, Barbara G. *The Women's Encyclopedia of Myths and Secrets*. Edison, New Jersey: Castle Books, 1996.

Waring, Philippa. *A Dictionary of Omens and Superstitions*. London: Souvenir Press, 1978.

Index

About the Author

Gerina Dunwich (whose first name is pronounced "Jereena") is a practicing Witch, an ordained minister (Universal Life Church), and a respected spokesperson for the Pagan community. She considers herself to be a lifelong student of the occult arts and is the author of numerous books on the spellcasting arts and the earth-oriented religion of Wicca. Her most popular titles include *Exploring Spellcraft, The Wicca Spellbook, Wicca Craft, The Pagan Book of Halloween, Wicca Candle Magick, Everyday Wicca, Wicca Love Spells,* and *Your Magickal Cat.*

Born under the sign of Capricorn with an Aries rising and her moon in Sagittarius, Gerina is also a professional astrologer and Tarot reader whose diverse clientele include a number of Hollywood celebrities and fellow occult authors. She is the High Priestess of the Coven of the Dark Shadows (formerly Coven Mandragora), and is the founder of the Bast-Wicca tradition, the Pagan Poets Society, and the Wheel of Wisdom School. Gerina is also a poet and a cat-lover. She writes and plays music and has lived in various parts of world, including a 300-year-old Colonial house near Salem, Massachusetts, and a haunted Victorian mansion in upstate New York. Her interests include herbal folklore, mythology, spiritualism, divination, dreamwork, hypnotism, and past-life regression. Gerina currently lives in Southern California with her Gemini soul mate and their feline familiars.

Gerina Dunwich's Web sites
The Mystical, Magickal World of Gerina Dunwich
http://www.gerinadunwich.com

Gerina Dunwich's Cauldron
http://clubs.yahoo.com/clubs/gerinadunwichscauldron

Gerina's Grimoire
http://iamawitch.com/freepages/grimoire

The Pagan Poets Society
http://clubs.yahoo.com/clubs/paganpoetssociety